Loblolly House

Elements of a
New Architecture

Stephen Kieran

James Timberlake

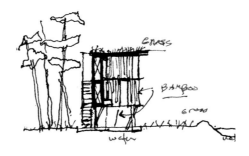

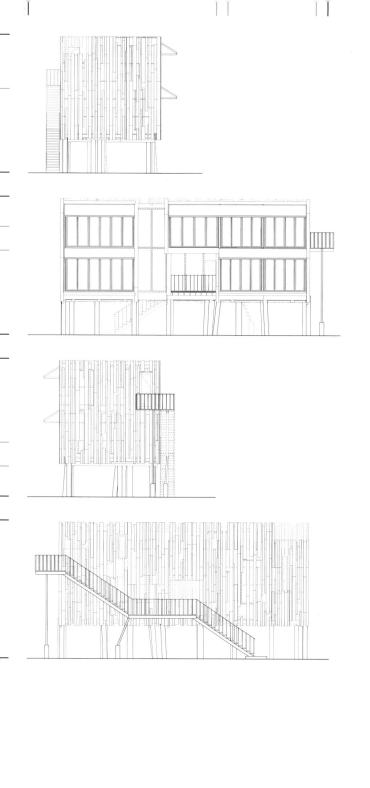

Loblolly House

Elements of a New Architecture

Stephen Kieran

James Timberlake

Preface by Barry Bergdoll
Introduction by Michael Stacey

Princeton Architectural Press

For Barbara, the best client an architect could ever desire

Published by
Princeton Architectural Press
37 East Seventh Street
New York, New York 10003

For a free catalog of books, call 1.800.722.6657.
Visit our website at www.papress.com.

Editor: Laurie Manfra
Designer: Jan Haux

Special thanks to: Nettie Aljian, Sara Bader, Dorothy Ball, Janet Behning,
Kristin Carlson, Becca Casbon, Penny (Yuen Pik) Chu, Russell Fernandez,
Pete Fitzpatrick, Wendy Fuller, Clare Jacobson, Aileen Kwun, Nancy
Eklund Later, Linda Lee, Katharine Myers, Lauren Nelson Packard, Jennifer
Thompson, Arnoud Verhaeghe, Paul Wagner, Joseph Weston, and Deb Wood
of Princeton Architectural Press—Kevin C. Lippert, publisher

Library of Congress Cataloging-in-Publication Data
Kieran, Stephen, 1951-
Loblolly House : elements of a new architecture / by Stephen Kieran and
James Timberlake ; foreword by Barry Bergdoll ; introduction by Michael Stacey.
p. cm.
ISBN 978-1-56898-747-7 (hardcover : alk. paper)
1. Loblolly House (Md.) 2. Kieran, Stephen, 1951–Homes and haunts–
Maryland–Taylors Island (Dorchester County : Island) 3. Prefabricated
houses–Maryland–Taylors Island (Dorchester County : Island) 4. Modular
construction–Maryland–Taylors Island (Dorchester County : Island)
I. Timberlake, James, 1952- II. Title.
NA7235.M32T39 2008
728.7'20975227–dc22
                                            2007051800

Loblolly House
Project team: Stephen Kieran, James Timberlake, David Riz,
    Marilia Rodrigues, Johnathan Ferrari, Alex Gauzza,
    Jeff Goldstein, Shawn Protz, George Ristow, Mark Rhoads
Fabrication and assembly: Bensonwood Homes
Construction: Arena Program Management
Structural engineer: CVM Structural Engineers
Mechanical, electrical, and plumbing engineer:
    Bruce Brooks & Associates
Civil engineer: Lane Engineering
Geotechnical engineer: John D. Hynes & Associates
Interiors: Marguerite Rodgers
Landscape design: Barbara Seymour Landscapes

Contents

Preface

Barry Bergdoll

For nearly two decades Stephen Kieran and James Timberlake have conducted their practice—today, numbering some fifty architects and collaborators in their Philadelphia office—as a sustained research project, delving into the very fundamentals of building. Although their position in architectural practice and thinking is generally aligned with the growing interest in prefabrication, each of their built projects defies categorization into the field's current typologies of flat pack, modular, or the numerous practices that hybridize the two. In their seminal book *Refabricating Architecture,* KieranTimberlake reframed the very question of prefabrication. In a holistic way they returned to the modernist tradition of reinventing the practice and language of architecture through off-site factory fabrication of building components. The issues they engaged extended well beyond deployable inventions and evolving fabrication systems to considerations of sustainability, site sensitivity, and to a philosophy of architecture and building.

The fact that all of their projects look different, even as their analyses continue to gain subtlety, refinement, and large-scale applicability, demonstrates that to think in terms of prefabrication does not mean to create built diagrams. Although this beautifully documented book follows the conception, fabrication, and rapid assembly of Loblolly House, one might almost say that the installation of a singularly beautiful and refined prefabricated house on a fragile shoreline site is in itself exemplary of how their processes are capable of producing highly inflected, personalized, and subtle works of architecture. Loblolly House is a singular accomplishment precisely because it is at once site specific and paradigmatic. It takes its place among the accomplishments of modern house design for its architectural qualities of transparency, its expression of construction methods and materials, and its lightweight enclosure of volumes, as well as for its fulfillment of one of the key dreams of modernism: the production of a factory-built architecture that parallels, even rivals, modernity's other industrial products, from cars to airplanes and appliances. Loblolly House fulfills the aspiration of rethinking architecture in terms of new means of industrial production and organized communication within a digital environment. It reveals, too, that architecture, conceived as a product, can be customized for an individual client and a specific site without compromising the clarity of its union of design and fabrication, thereby putting to rest two of the oldest anxieties about factory-made architecture.

The current explosion of interest in digital parametrics runs the risk of accentuating form for form's sake, leading to the architect's gradual abstraction into the algorithms of design rather than the logic of making. Central to KieranTimberlake's philosophy is the belief that digital parametrics hold the promise for a large-scale realignment of design and fabrication. Rather than distance the architect ever further from the actual making of things, digital tools have the possibility of creating a hand-to-glove relationship between design and fabrication, between the testing ground and the conditions of construction and natures of materials. In short, Kieran-Timberlake's questioning of the division of intellect and labor is characteristic of architecture's very rise as a profession, one that saw the designer progressively removed from the stone yard and timber mill.

In the new realm of computer-enabled mass customization, the architect's earliest conceptions begin with the possibilities of building and the nature of contemporary fabrication. This was a dream that Konrad Wachsmann and Walter Gropius pursued for decades, with notoriously disappointing results. Like Wachsmann, Kieran-Timberlake's research often leads to a concentration on the joint, a logical necessity of a system that seeks to eliminate wet assembly and extensive site work; but the comparison ends there. Just as the automotive and aviation industries have radically transformed in recent years, so might architectural fabrication move toward a system of subassemblies and greater coordination of just-in-time, robotic delivery of highly differentiated products ready for deft hand-assembly, be these cars, planes, or houses. If *prefabrication* once implied a radical simplification, so that within a Wachsmann house the same panel could be used in the horizontal and vertical planes as a wall, floor, or ceiling, KieranTimberlake's approach introduces the possibility for complex and diverse elements to be assembled into blocks or chunks prior to delivery on site. The combination of what they call "highly serviced blocks" with structural frames is a return to the old modernist separation of frame and infill, or served and servant, as their distant mentor Louis Kahn defined it decades before Kieran and Timberlake arrived at the University of Pennsylvania and reconsidered that separation in terms of the organization of information and streams of assembly, as seen in other manufacturing sectors, today. The ideal might be the construction of a building the way BMW manufactures cars in its recently completed Leipzig plant designed by Zaha Hadid: each car is a distinct, customized object made up of complex sets of parts and subassemblies. But KieranTimberlake is not content to catch up with the car industry a century after Ford introduced the assembly line. Refusing the whole tradition of types in both classical architectural theory and in the logic of standardization, they hope that the age of information technology will provide the means by which the constructive language of architecture—realized by them in aluminum, glass, and polycarbonate, as well as traditional timber—will provide standardized and optimized elements for a continually renewed act of design. Certainly, the sober beauty and elegance of Loblolly House is a highly promising substantiation of that philosophy.

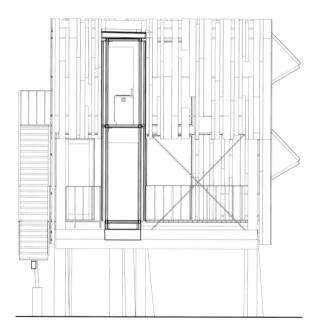

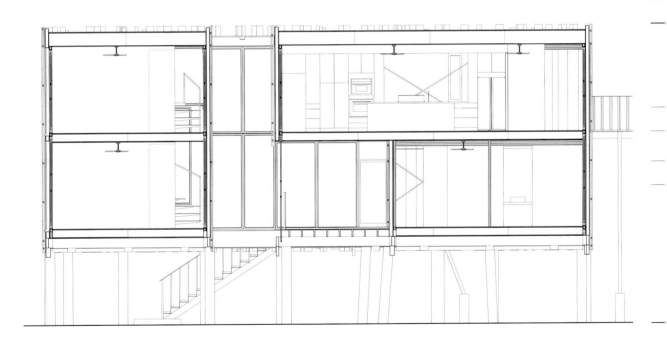

Introduction

Michael Stacey

Stephen Kieran and James Timberlake are two of the most thoughtful practitioners of architecture working in America today. In their lives they combine practice, research, and teaching. Following in the footsteps of Louis Kahn, they lead a final year research studio at the University of Pennsylvania School of Design. Their constructed projects display a depth of understanding of the art and craft of architecture. In their hands, theory and practice are a single realm, as was ably demonstrated in their 2002 book, *Manual.*

Their practice, KieranTimberlake Associates, is based in Philadelphia and at its core is an active engagement with the means and methods of construction and a committment to research, which they actively deploy in their architecture. From the layered facade of Levine Hall and the aluminum structure of the SmartWrap pavilion, their office has cultivated a strong component culture. The origins of Loblolly House can be traced to research undertaken for the Latrobe Prize, which lead to the publication of *Refabricating Architecture* in 2003.

Kieran and Timberlake's interest in prefabrication appears to have arisen from the careful craftsmanship exhibited in their earlier work, as well as from their pursuit of quality and refusal to accept the current norms of the North American construction industry. There is nothing rhetorical about their architecture; it demonstrates their commitment to solving the key issues that humankind faces in the twenty-first century.

After peeling back the layers of Loblolly House's west facade, you can sit in the living space and benefit from a totally unobstructed view of the Chesapeake Bay and distant sea and sky. Gasholders on the far shore remind you of civilization's impact on this land. Before 1000 BCE the fertile grounds that surround this estuary were farmed by Native Americans. With the establishment of the first New World settlement on the James River at the turn of the seventeenth century, the region was colonized by the British.

Looking west toward the setting sun and the nation's capital, the house is an eloquent critique of the United States' nonparticipation in the Kyoto Protocol and further evidence that we need not take to earth-sheltered bunkers to engage the pressing issue of climate change. The quality of the design of our homes, schools, and places of work can provide a more sustainable ecology, as evidenced in Loblolly House.

When the adjustable west facade is in the open position, the section *is* the architecture. Each room not only has a view of the bay, it becomes part of the landscape, and this connectivity is further enhanced by the height of the inhabitable spaces. The potential to sleep or study under the stars links this house to precedents of the modern movement: Richard Neutra's Lovell Health House in Los Angeles and J. Duiker's Openluchtschool in Amsterdam.

As the largest estuary in the United States, the Chesapeake Bay retains significant biodiversity despite the consequences of human ingenuity, be these intended or not, from activities such as hunting and manufacturing. In 1639 Maryland established game laws to protect certain species of birds, including the great blue heron. Homeowners Stephen and Barbara clearly value the ecosystems of the bay. The polycarbonate screens on the west facade take inspiration from local duck blinds, without recourse to hunting. The use of prefabricated components to enclose the sophisticated building systems minimized the impact of construction on the site.

Resting in this wooded landscape, the house itself seems to touch the ground only lightly, and the site below is already being reclaimed by indigenous species.

Even though Loblolly House is located in Taylors Island, Maryland, below the Mason Dixon Line, where summertime temperatures peak in excess of 100 degrees Fahrenheit with relative humidity averaging at 75 percent, it has been designed with minimal need for mechanical air-conditioning. This energy-hungry invention is one of the major reasons why America's carbon footprint is four times the world average. We need to uninvent this technology and learn to provide comfort without relying on petroleum-based energy sources. Loblolly House is a bold step on this journey. KieranTimberlake is monitoring the performance of its adjustable facade, which preheats the air in winter and provides shade and ventilation in summer. The budgets of many modern buildings are dominated by the costs of services, but creating comfort via the building fabric returns the investment to the visible architecture and reduces the demand for energy.

Loblolly House is not only a statement in favor of a more ecological approach, it is an essay in prefabrication that exemplifies KieranTimberlake's engagement with craft, industry, and manufacturing. The new techniques they utilize, including scaffolding, blocks, and cartridges, are described in detail in this book. Loblolly House demonstrates that prefabrication has the greatest possibility of success when used in a hybrid manner, combining the advantages of highly serviced blocks with structural frames. The spaces created within a home should not be limited by the dimensions of production or the maximum sizes of transported goods. Nevertheless, prefabrication will evolve into an established construction method in the twenty-first century because it is an effective means for delivering quality while minimizing waste. Construction need not resemble trench warfare—it can be carried out in the controlled environment of a factory. For example, Loblolly relies on *floor* and *wall cartridges*. The floor cartridges, which contain prebuilt service systems, are considered "smart"—they were simply plugged in by the carpenters at Bensonwood Homes. It is an example of building services nearing the simplicity of an Apple computer: a plug-and-play architecture.

The timber piles that elevate the house are not the rhetorical *piloti* of the modern movement. Because the house is sited on the shore of a barrier island, they are essential for flood protection. The piles were driven into the ground at diverse angles, as is the norm in many jetties. If the architects had listened to the piles, they would be orthogonal, because as they were driven into the ground, many sought to become vertical. A kind of engineered timber called Kerto was then used to transfer structural loads between the rough-hewn piles and precise aluminum framing.

Loblolly House is a rare example of a multistory structure that utilizes aluminum as the primary material. Since the 1950s, aluminum has been the metal of choice for curtain wall substructures. In Europe, 52 percent of it is produced using hydroelectricity, significantly reducing its embodied energy, and 92 percent is recovered when buildings are demolished. Recycled aluminum uses only 5 percent of the energy traditionally needed to win it from bauxite. Used wisely, it can be a very sustainable metal.

Professor Colin Davies, author of *The Prefabricated Home*, might judge the success of Loblolly on whether it remains a prototype or is made into a product that can be adapted to many locations. Stephen and James are working with LivingHomes to develop such a system. Market-driven architecture, especially housing, too often lapses into the lowest common denominator, but product-based architecture should remain thoughtful and offer new and well-considered opportunities to the North American housing market.

Upon entering Stephen and Barbara's shoreside residence I was struck by how delightful it is. In a world filled with so much banality—I had driven past miles of enormous detached houses, each with at least one SUV parked outside—the beauty of this site-specific home is satisfying in itself. It reminded me of John Winter's review, published in 1976, of Michael and Patty Hopkins' house in Hampstead, London, where he observed, "This is their home and not housing." The contribution of Barbara, as client, and the advice of Marguerite Rodgers on the interior design parallels the creative influence of Margaret and Frances Macdonald in the work of Charles Rennie Mackintosh.

Loblolly House gains its authenticity from the integration of space, structure, and adjustable environmental systems. Though crafted from aluminum, timber, glass, and polycarbonate, it shares a kinship with the arts-and-crafts homes of Greene and Greene in its exposed structural elements and in its acceptance of materials. Loblolly House is not a slick, super-product of surface architecture. The architects were searching for substance, not style.

The inventive facade combines two standard products, polycarbonate-clad hangar doors and double-glazed patio doors, both of which slide and fold, dematerializing the facade almost effortlessly. In comparison, the eighty-foot-wide retractable plate-glass window used by Mies van der Rohe in the Tugendhat House seems like an act of tectonic drama. Distinguishing these houses is an eighty-year period of dynamic technological development, which included the invention of polycarbonate in 1953.

Kieran and Timberlake have not fallen into the trap of formalism that has enmeshed so many contemporary architects. A 1:1000 scale model of the house reveals just how carefully they conceived the proportions and nuances, such as the cutout that facilitates access to the roof. The house was designed using a building information model (BIM) to define the components, though it is the pixelated aesthetic of the timber rainscreen that is most suggestive of the use of computers. This cladding, which camouflages the house among the loblolly pines, truly reflects the tools and era in which it was designed.

Prior to founding their own studio, Stephen and James both worked at the office of Robert Venturi and Denise Scott Brown from the late 1970s to the early '80s, but after a visit to Loblolly House, a guest may well believe they had worked in the office of Charles and Ray Eames. One finds no trace of the quirkiness or graphic postmodern aesthetic of Venturi and Scott Brown, as in the Vanna Venturi House, built in 1962. If any connection can be made to architects of British origin, it is to be found in the influence of Louis Kahn on Richard Rogers, Norman Foster, and Michael Hopkins. Philosophically, the house appears to be informed more by Reyner Banham's *Architecture of the Well-tempered Environment* than by Venturi and Scott Brown's *Complexity and Contradiction in Architecture*. Nevertheless, Loblolly House risks being misunderstood in the same way that Charles and Ray Eames' 1949 Case Study House #8 has been misunderstood. Sure, it is assembled predominantly from components that anyone can find in a catalog, but like the Eames House, it is a wonderful demonstration of the architects' skill in crafting a family- and site-specific home.

In *Refabricating Architecture*, Kieran and Timberlake bemoaned the construction industry for being asleep for the last eighty years. Coincidentally, eighty years have also passed since the publication of Le Corbusier's *Towards a New Architecture*. While most industries have benefited from the technological inventiveness of the last century, construction enterprises have sleepwalked into a counterproductive state of mediocrity characterized by the American architect's active disengagement from the means and methods of building. Enshrined in the American Institute of Architects' standard Form of Appointment is language establishing the avoidance of risk, which essentially has translated into losses of opportunity and authorship. Kieran and Timberlake are proposing a way to deliver quality architecture at a reasonable cost and in less time, through the use of prefabricated building components.

Their last book ended with a call to arms: "We invite the world of construction to begin anew with these processes that can make everyone's world and the architect's work better." The vision presented was rather corporate, with houses being built by a worldwide assembler, such as Boeing. Through Loblolly House, completed in 2006, Kieran and Timberlake have demonstrated their commitment to ecologically responsible architecture. Working closely with the fabricators and builders at Bensonwood Homes, they have delivered on the argument set forth in *Refabricating Architecture*, and the reality has proven more promising than the polemic. Unlike 1960s mass housing, the reality is no longer corporate. It's personal, and it is delivered with authenticity.

Provocation

Stephen Kieran

The environment has co-opted sustainability. Just as concerning as the environment, less recognized, and even less acted upon are the escalating costs and declining quality of design and construction. By equating sustainability with the environment, we limit our ability to advance a truly robust plan of environmental reparation. The rising cost of construction (disproportionate to the rest of the economy), the ongoing decline in the craft and quality of architecture, and the daily damage our buildings inflict upon the environment represent a daunting confluence of forces for change. In this challenge, we see great opportunity. Unseen synergies between these factors—quality, affordability, and the environment—offer a broadly based agenda for a more sustainable way forward. And they formed the aspiration for the design, fabrication, and assembly of Loblolly House.

The profession of architecture is in the midst of a crisis of confidence, both in the capacity and the desire to realize much needed improvements in productivity and efficiency. If we continue to ignore the industry's needs, we do so at our own peril. With each passing year the affordability crisis worsens. Construction costs continue to outpace the general economy by a factor of two-, three-, and sometimes four-to-one, creating an inflationary spiral, year in and year out. With every 1 percent increase, more people are denied access to quality housing and home ownership. Underlying these economic realities is the fact that productivity throughout the design and construction industries has been on the decline for the last several decades. While other sectors of the nonfarm economy have experienced gains in productivity of more than 80 percent over the past forty years, ours has witnessed a 20 percent drop. Compared to the rest of the economy, this 100 percent swing—with other industries experiencing 80 percent growth and ours a 20 percent setback—is not only unacceptable, it's unsustainable.

Once synonymous with quality craftsmanship and symbolizing the highest levels of human achievement, our buildings are, more often than not, seen by the public as bastions of mediocrity. With each passing year, the litany of problems associated with incomplete, incorrect, or poor workmanship grows longer. In most cases, quality is applied after the fact, if at all. This method of operation is built into the existing process, with a "fix it later" work ethic and a "talk the owner and designer into accepting the compromises, because we are behind schedule and over budget" approach to problem solving. Only occasionally is quality deeply and intelligently embedded within design and construction processes. The consequences of these inadequacies spill over, rather dramatically, into another realm: that of our responsibility to be stewards of the natural environment. For example, poorly designed and improperly installed cladding systems abound, leading to increased air infiltration and unmanageable moisture transfer through exterior walls. The result: additional and unnecessary energy expenditure and subquality indoor air. These problems are further compounded when substandard cladding systems are coupled with maximum horsepower building systems designed to compensate for the building envelope's unpredictable performance.

The ecological footprint that we leave on the natural world continues to deepen. If we proceed with business as usual, the consequences of this footprint will escalate. Growing worldwide populations will demand more of the world's natural resources, including water, energy, air, and raw materials. Mitigating the environmental impact associated with this rise in demand remains the focus of many environmental groups. While their efforts are beneficial, they do little more than offset the already enlarged footprint associated with our expanding population. In truth, our paradigms of consumption must change, if only to repair the damage exacted over the past few decades.

The mandate of sustainability is threefold: improve the productivity of design and construction, enhance affordability and quality, and do so in an ethical and aesthetically moving manner. This mandate is not optional. Increasingly, our clients demand it, and the people who use our architecture deserve it. The question for all engaged in design and construction is whether we have the desire, insight, and resourcefulness to seize the challenge that the current crisis affords. Sustainability's three main objectives—cost, quality, and the environment—are interdependent. Instead of prolonging our current paralysis, we must seek ways of understanding how these crises connect, rather than confound.

Since there are few models of efficiency in our own industry, we must look elsewhere for solutions. In the early 1990s the automotive industry faced a similar crisis of productivity and responded with a swift and expansive restructuring of its design and fabrication processes. By 1990 the 4,000 parts that evolved from the Model T to compose the contemporary automobile came together one by one at the factory. Over a remarkably short period of time, these production methodologies were reconstituted as subsets of fifteen or fewer integrated component assemblies, each fabricated by external suppliers who assisted in the design. For example, the more than 200 parts that made up a dashboard were collapsed into a single, integrated component with quick-couple connections for attachment at the point of final assembly. Instead of a single point of focus for the assembly of all 4,000 parts, the process was dispersed, allowing for multiple centers of focused design, innovation, and production. Each integrated component undergoes its own quality control prior to arriving at the main plant. Owing to the fact that substantially fewer joints were arriving at the final point of assembly, it became possible to enhance quality control for the few remaining connections. The results of this redesign process were higher productivity, lower cost, and improved quality. In lieu of the sequential, part-by-part weaving together of an automobile, the process is now conceived as a quilt of integrated components.

Toyota, of course, became the master of these new strategies. Underlying the design and production of their vehicles is a set of beliefs aligned with the current mandate of sustainability. At a time when most American automotive manufacturers are under competitive assault, Toyota is thriving precisely because it has comprehensively dealt with these challenges. Intrinsic to their practice is a relentless focus on the process itself. Individual outcomes (automobiles) are seen as stages within a never-ending effort at self-improvement. Within their design philosophy the concept of a static type and the notion of perfection are irrelevant. Their culture insists upon ceaseless criticism and continual progress, driven by the ideals of better quality and enhanced design, delivered in less time and lower cost. More often, their processes are focused on environmental concerns, such as reducing

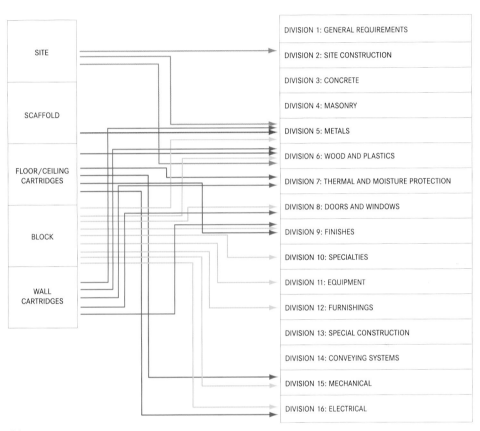

0.1

0.1
The 40,000 parts that make up the average
American house collapse into five integrated
construction elements

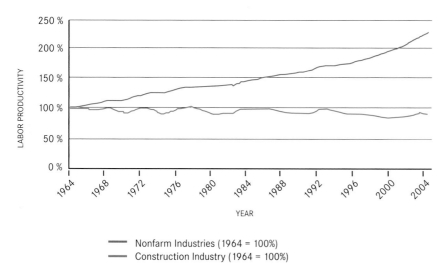

Construction and Nonfarm Labor Productivity Index

Nonfarm Industries (1964 = 100%)
Construction Industry (1964 = 100%)

Reference: Paul Teicholz, PhD, Professor (Research) Emeritus, Dept of Civil and Environmental Engineering, Stanford University

0.2

0.2
Productivity losses in the construction industry
as compared to gains in other sectors of the
nonfarm economy

carbon emissions and improving fuel efficiency. As a result, Toyota not only possesses significant cost and quality advantages, but they have simultaneously become the worldwide leader in hybrid technology. Every member of the company participates in this neverending effort guided by a singular ethic of improvement, with many of the design, production, and environmental process innovations, big and small alike, initiating with workers, not with management.

In contrast to the fields of industrial design and manufacturing, architecture and construction have been devoid of substantive change. Except for a few isolated gains in productivity, the overall trend has been downward, resulting in escalating cost and declining quality. Energy consumption continues to rise, with little regard for water and material conservation. In fact, according to the National Association of Homebuilders, a recent study revealed that the typical American house consists of more than 40,000 parts, most of which arrive one by one at the site for field erection, stick by stick.

If 80 percent of an automobile consists of integrated component assemblies built away from the point of final assembly, then the American house is its polar opposite, with more than 80 percent of its parts coming together at the site to which they are anchored. The time and costs associated with building a home increase as more systems are added. These expenditures stand in contrast to the productivity gains realized by other industries, where integrated, prefabricated assemblies are the norm. Meanwhile, with respect to quality, architecture and construction's failure to innovate is even worse. A study conducted in Florida found that more than 40 percent of new homes have "significant quality flaws."

It is widely known that average household energy use in the United States can be as much as four times that of other developed nations. According to a University of Michigan analysis, the conventional developer-built house will consume more than 15,000 gigajoules of energy over a life cycle of fifty years. This figure could be decreased *right now*, not five years from now, to 5,000 gigajoules, using existing design and fabrication strategies. The fragmented nature of the housing industry, however, works against any efforts to diffuse the skills, knowledge, and resources necessary to realize sizable reductions in energy use. Judging by the integration strategies adopted by other industries, the means for acheiving higher productivity is through controlled implementations that reduce the overall environmental footprint.

Our objectives for the design, fabrication, and assembly of Loblolly House were as follows: create a house that evokes the extraordinary natural world that is its home; then redesign the process of design and construction, embedding within it an environmental ethic that privileges efficiency and quality. The central tool underlying our process was a parametric building information model (BIM), which provided the level of geometric certainty needed to shift the paradigm of design from a sequential, gravity-driven construction process to a simultaneous prefabrication process with integrated components and on-site assembly. Like automobiles, ships, and aircraft, Loblolly House was first built as a virtual artifact. This simulation was the mechanism that enabled simultaneity. The site no longer served as the factory, and nearly 70 percent of the effort shifted to off-site integration and fabrication. Our long-term objective, however is to altogether obliterate the Construction Specifications Institute's ever expanding system of nomenclature. Today, nearly fifty divisions of materials and equipment classify tens of thousands of products into a confusing and disjointed array of parts. In its place, we propose to simplify, merge, and unify these materials and environmental systems—structures, windows, doors, and finishes—into integrated assemblies, which we consider to be the *elements* of a new architecture.

Just as the site inspires an elemental house derived from nature, so does the process inspire a return to an elemental architecture, almost classical in its nomenclature: scaffold, cartridge, block, fixture, furnishing, and equipment. The 40,000 parts of the conventional American house—spanning fifty CSI divisions—collapse into several component types, ready for site assembly. With this new focus on integrated components, there are fewer joints. Quality, craftsmanship, and performance are greatly improved. While the existing on-site practices for home construction remain dispersed among thousands of small-scale builders (who lack knowledge of or access to best-practice environmental initiatives), a limited number of well capitalized, off-site integrators could provide leading-edge environmental components across the housing market. Essentially, these players will redefine the housing supply chain in the United States.

In this new paradigm, construction is no longer a linear, ground-up process but an integrated and simultaneous effort. Off-site fabricated elements are integrated hierarchically into cartridges, blocks, panels, and equipment while on-site work, including foundations and utilities, is underway. Fabrication and assembly replace construction, increasing productivity and quality while decreasing the environmental footprint.

Loblolly House is a provocation to seize the sustainability challenge by focusing on productivity, quality, and our need to forge a symbiotic relationship with the natural world. Its design and assembly mark our firm's passage from desire to deed.

1.1

1.1
A northwest view of Loblolly House, looking
through the loblolly pines

Place

Named after the pine trees that populate its site on the Chesapeake Bay, Loblolly House seeks to unite nature with architectural form. Positioned between a dense grove of pines, a foreground of profuse cordgrass, and the shore of the bay, the home forms itself within the existing landscape of sea, horizon, sky, and setting sun. The landscape is elemental. The eye sweeps upward, from the varying hues of the tall grasses to the columnar pines. Across the bay and toward the horizon, shifting hues of blue and gray continually transform the sky. Time is marked by the daily passage of the sun, as it sets directly to the west. Like an Ellsworth Kelly painting, the colors define an ever shifting range, with the setting sun ritualistically adding a burst of orange as it punctuates the end of each day.

Loblolly House is not just set within the natural elements, it is extracted from the site's ecology. This distinction is suggested by the comparison of two sculptures from different periods and cultures: the Bronze Warrior from the Sea of Riace, a Greek statue dating to 460 BCE, and the Aztec Eagle Warrior, dating to 1440–1469 CE. The Greek statue stands alone, a formidable and confi-

dent warrior. The Aztec figure shows man as a hybrid creature, part human and part raptor, with the human body emerging out of animate form. At work here are two divergent interpretations of man's place in the natural world. The Greek warrior stands distinct from nature. The Aztec figure is inextricably woven through it; man and nature are inseparable, with each providing context for the other. In architectural terms, Loblolly House seeks a relationship to nature like that of the Aztec sculpture. It seeks to exist within the elements of site and it aspires to create an aesthetic connection to the ecology that surrounds it. Conceived as a hybrid, it is derived from the elements of nature but organized through the artifice of architecture.

A comparison between Loblolly House and Mies van der Rohe's Farnsworth House illustrates, in architectural terms, the differing relationships to nature that these two sculptures embody. While both are elevated on platforms, the Farnsworth House exists as an object in a field. Enclosed in glass and organized around a central core, its form is independent of nature, not a derivation of it. By contrast, Loblolly House is a viewing

1.2
Bronze Warrior from the Sea of Riace, ca. 460 BCE

1.3
Aztec Eagle Warrior, ca. 1440–1469 CE

1.2   1.3

platform set within the trees. Lifted on canted timber piles, which rise from the earth to support the platform, the house opens itself to the elements. Owing to its elevated height, it is both secure and precarious. The viewing platform within the trees is a blind, not a fishbowl. Open to the water and setting sun, its sweeping views extend across the Chesapeake Bay. Almost fully sheathed on the north, south, and east sides, it is single-minded in its focus. Boards of red cedar extend across the side and rear facades, overlapping windows and cement sheathing while drawing surrounding patterns of light from the forest onto and into the house.

The passage to Loblolly House begins at the bridge from the mainland. A two-lane road winds past a campground, a dock for crab boats, a shanty, the local grill, the post office, and the fire station. Beyond this landing, habitation thins to the occasional cottage or small farm set between marshes. Two miles from the bridgehead and opposite an open field, an 800-foot-long driveway pierces the loblolly forest to the east. From this narrow road, the bay and sky come into focus, with the house offset to the north. The rear and side facades appear as a camouflage pattern, gradually emerging. As you draw closer, the pattern becomes more distinct. The vertical cladding is illuminated from behind by windows that, from the inside, appear as if peering through the forest itself. During the afternoon hours, as the sun moves around to the west, the orange glass footbridge burns brightly through the cedar slats at the house's core, emphasizing the sun's role in this fusion of nature and architecture. With the sun to the east, the forest mirrors itself in the large windows as reflections of actual loblolly pines mingle with the house's surface representations.

Movement inside the house repeats the natural elements encountered along this passage. The driveway ends beneath the house, where timber piles lift it above the cordgrass plane. A small bamboo garden encloses the driveway, and a plank walkway divides the shoots of bamboo. In architectural terms, the entryway restates the experience of driving through the forest. Open to the sky, the atrium at the core of the house is emblematic of this passage. Upon passing through the bamboo court, you ascend the stairs along the exterior of the east facade as you make your way to an aerial platform.

1.4
Farnsworth House, Ludwig Mies van der Rohe, architect, completed 1951

1.5
Loblolly House, KieranTimberlake Associates, architect, completed 2006

1.4   1.5

1.6

1.6
Dense cordgrass and loblolly pines line the
shoreside site on the Chesapeake Bay

1.7

1.8

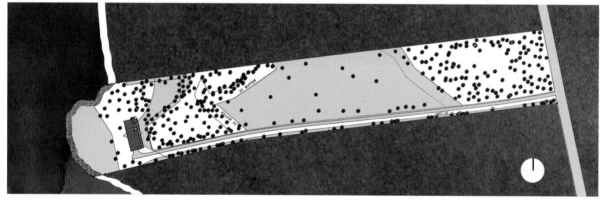

1.9

1.7
The site's two pre-existing structures

1.8
A view of the bay from the proposed site of
the house

1.9
Bird's-eye plan depicting the elongated
driveway and proliferation of loblolly pines

At the first landing, an almost cavernous opening set back from the wall, provides access to the two bedrooms on the first level. The shadow of this recessed entryway contrasts with the bridge's orange wall, juxtaposing the deeply sheltered door and the adjacent glass. Ascending the second landing, you arrive at the front door. Unlike the recessed entryway on the first level, this square platform projects like the osprey nests that populate the island. From here, you can touch the trunk and canopy of an adjacent loblolly tree before entering the main room, a dining and living space centered around a kitchen island. The west wall opens to the bay, and narrow full-height windows on the north and south walls provide slivers of views to the surrounding forest. Passing across the great room's green bamboo floors to a small exterior atrium, a glass footbridge with bamboo on both sides divides the court once again, separating forest from architecture. On the right, orange glass juxtaposes a view of the bay, visible through the west atrium. The ceiling of the footbridge is painted a deep, dusky sky blue, and the green bamboo floor extends the cordgrass plane. It is here that the site's natural elements join with the architecture: grass becomes floor, sky becomes ceiling, and sun and trees become walls. Across the atrium and beyond the footbridge (on the second level) is one of two guest bedrooms. A spiral stair connects this room to an identical one below it and leads to a shared bathroom on a midlevel landing. On the first level, a canopied deck (beneath the living room) extends the master bedroom to the outside.

Loblolly House is conceived as nature woven through architecture. Simultaneously, it is porch *and* hearth. If shelter exists as a filter to separate man from the elements, then Loblolly House seeks to challenge the former distinction between ecology and the artifice of man.

1.10

1.10
The east facade, as approached from the driveway

1.11
The recessed entrance on the first level

1.13

1.12
Orange glass illuminates the house from behind
the cedar slats, evoking the setting sun

1.13
Twilight view of the west facade

1.14

1.14
The covered deck outside the master bedroom

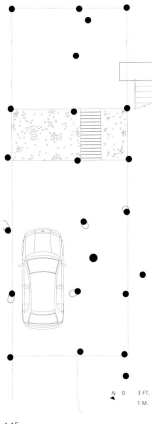

1.15
Ground level

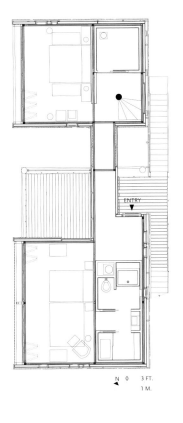

ENTRY

N 0   3 FT.
        1 M.

1.16
First level

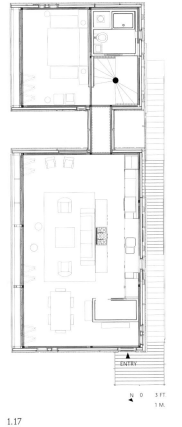

ENTRY

N 0   3 FT.
        1 M.

1.17
Second level

Overleaf:
1.18
Second-level dining and living area, with one
section of the adjustable facade open

Simulation,
not representation

What if both the architect and builder conceived and built *forward*? What if we no longer were to think backward from the first image of form so that conceiving and building could proceed in unison, not competition? In earlier and less complex times, vernacular forms and methods governed much of our thinking, drawing, and making. With the current complexity of programs and building systems, the new tools of today promise to rejoin our processes of thinking and making. The drawing tool of which we speak is parametric modeling and the wider set of integrated software tools referred to as building information modeling (BIM).

Despite the integration of computers within the field of architecture more than twenty-five years ago, the drawing types we use to describe our buildings have changed little since the Renaissance. Each exists by itself as an artifact. Each represents architecture at a particular time and place and from a particular point of view, be it a plan, section, elevation, or detail. Depicting even a small portion of a building requires many images, and there are important junctures and changes in plane that remain unexamined until construction is underway. In short, our tools have been static and incomplete. They represent architecture but do not simulate it. In contrast, parametric drawing tools allow for the formation of a solid model grounded in the physical elements that make up our architecture. These elements exist in the model independent of point of view and can be extracted and viewed in the round. Elements as miniscule as individual screws are set within a hierarchy of increasingly larger elements.

The parametric model is built like the building, from virtual elements that correspond to the physical building. In essence, we are building our architecture virtually before we do so physically. The parametric model becomes the prototype, with the finished architecture benefiting from its precursor.

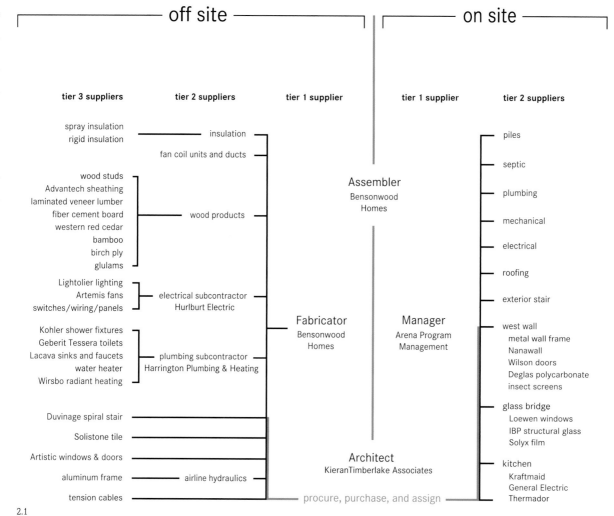

2.1

2.1
Redesigned supply-chain diagram

Process

Before the fundamental processes of architecture can change, we must focus ourselves anew. We must return to the process of thinking, drawing, and making. We must begin by not beginning. We must resist the irresistible: the instinct to seek form. The first act of design is to *not do* what the client has invited us to do. The first act is not the thing itself but the process of thinking and making. Nowadays, we pursue form and then describe the desired outcome in disembodied or, as contractors would say, "disemboweled" drawings and specifications. Reams of disaggregated plans, details, words, and numbers provide the puzzle, not the path, between intention and form. This puzzle, complete with detail keys embedded within detail keys and references set within references, is handed to others to discern and construct. If we are lucky, we get to keep ourselves on the job all the way through construction, acting as interpreters and arbiters of what we really intended but neither foresaw nor conveyed. All the while, as the instructions that lie between intention and outcome become obscure, we bemoan the ongoing decline in productivity, quality, and control.

Thinking is the hardest part of beginning, because conceiving architecture and building it are not parallel processes. The manner of conception is such that we do not build the building first with our minds, eyes, and hands. Rather, we begin with the vision of a hoped-for outcome. Then we deconstruct the desire articulated in our schematic vision into thousands of disjointed drawings and words that serve as the legal documents for establishing cost. Contractors and subcontractors guess at our intentions with product submittals, shop drawings, and occasional efforts at coordinating the disciplines. Then collectively we revise and resubmit until everyone agrees that intention and form are aligned, that is, until we start to build. Subcontractors order materials and construct the building piece by piece from the ground up, measuring to fit each new circumstance to its predecessor. Meanwhile, the architect proceeds to answer question after question, sometimes numbering in the thousands, about what we really meant.

The process through which we conceive does not determine that which we make. It does, however, propose opportunities, the first being a collaborative and meaningful

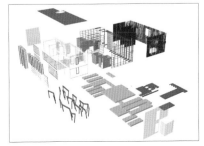

2.2

2.3

2.2
An early axonometric diagram of the house's prefabricated elements

2.3
Sketch from the journal of Marilia Rodrigues, project architect

synthesis of different kinds of expert knowledge. When architecture is simulated through parametric modeling, it becomes counterproductive, even painful, to work in a disaggregated manner, where each contributor produces separate design documents. The parametric model is not a representation of intention; intentionality is embedded within it. Instead of allowing for separate areas of responsibility, the model forces integration. Each collaborator—builder, owner, architect, engineer, fabricator, or supplier—contributes to a unified vision of a building to come, already simulated in the solid model. Structural and mechanical drawings are no longer segregated from architectural drawings. Product submittals, shop drawings, and coordination drawings no longer exist as independent information in need of coordination. All intention and design information resides in a single place: the parametric model.

Early on in the process, we understood the necessity of designing the supply chain and seeking out collaborators with whom we could build the house virtually before attempting it physically. The supply chain's basic outline required that we redesign all we had learned as architects. We knew that we had the tools necessary for the house's integrated assemblies to be fabricated off-site. At the same time, we were keenly aware of the very real differences between the architecture, engineering, and construction industries, on the one hand, and the automotive, aircraft, and shipbuilding industries that we had studied. The principle difference being, of course, that buildings are fastened to the ground. For this reason, we segregated the supply chain into off-site and onsite processes, with the two sets of activities proceeding simultaneously from opposite directions.

Architectural process design differs distinctly from the hierarchical, one-directional supply chains of our sister industries. We set out to find collaborators with whom we could extend our design and procurement efforts. Philadelphia-based contractor Arena Program Management agreed early on to provide site-based services. Finding the appropriate off-site fabricator, however, proved more difficult. Conversations with several Pennsylvania-based modular builders proved fruitless. Tedd Benson and his New Hampshire–based company, Bensonwood Homes, had been building timber frame homes for decades. Several years ago they had gone into the business of providing floor, roof, and wall panels. For our purposes, they were the ideal collaborator.

The aluminum scaffold system, which we were proposing to use as the frame, was not familiar to them. Like us, they had only just begun to integrate off-site fabrication systems, but they embraced our challenge. Most importantly, they stood out among American builders as the most comprehensive and advanced users of parametric modeling and computer aided manufacturing. Working together, we built a single parametric model of Loblolly House before it went into shop fabrication. The relationship between the project architect in our office, Marilia Rodrigues, and the staff at Bensonwood Homes, led by Tony Poanessa, Paul Boa, and Hans Porschitz, was intensely collaborative. While our office worked with Revit, Bensonwood developed the fabrication model in CadWorks version thirteen, with each party translating back and forth through AutoCAD. Though the tool for translating files was not perfect, it worked well enough and enabled communication. Coordination meetings between the builders, architects, and engineers involved large-scale projections that allowed everyone to navigate through details to examine conflicts and devise solutions. Even the structural, mechanical, plumbing, and electrical drawings were integrated into the model, allowing us to view system interfaces virtually, prior to construction. The parametric model then directly drove the Hundegger machine that measured, cut, drilled, and otherwise fabricated the wooden elements that composed a majority of the floors, walls, ceilings, and secondary structures within the house.

The model also invited us to describe the various parts that made up each element. This information is embedded within the solids, because precise dimensions, geometries, and profiles were integral to the model's formation. Some product suppliers were able to provide parametric details of their materials, which in the future will eliminate a central labor cost on the part of the architect engaged in the model's development. Much of the product information regarding structural properties, manufacturer product references, lead times, and dozens of other useful facts were readily present as annotated information in the parametric model.

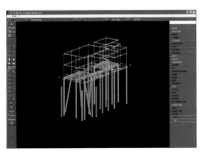

2.4
Screenshot of the CadWorks model used by
Bensonwood Homes

Steps 1–9

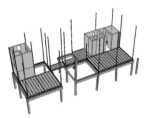  

2.5

2.5
An early diagram of the proposed assembly
sequence

Steps 10–18

In the future, it wouldn't be much of a leap to simplify or even eliminate major parts of the current submittal process for product information, fabrication, and coordination drawings. At a minimum, these no longer need to occur as separate events, independent of initiating drawings and specifications. The parametric model becomes the repository of *all* information, bringing with it significant advantages in quality control.

Upon completion, the model became the tool for managing the supply chain. Aluminum extrusions, for example, were created with embedded data, such as manufacturer and distributor information, model name, size of profile, length, and cost. Submittal and shop drawing processes became obsolete. Since these components had already been constructed virtually, we were able to accurately catalog sizes and quantities prior to submiting orders via email, using information derived from the parametric model. In effect, an entire segment of the design and construction process was eliminated; or, perhaps more appropriately, it was integrated into the model at an earlier stage in the design process.

Due to the dimensional certainty of the model, we were able to direct-purchase a number of building systems and assign them to either the off-site fabricator (Bensonwood Homes) or on-site builder (Arena Program Management). In addition to the aluminum scaffold, we ordered several other items directly. Wood-frame windows and doors were bought and assigned to Bensonwood for factory installation in wall cartridges. The folding doors made of aluminum and glass and the bifolding hangar doors and glazing elements that enclose the west facade were all purchased directly from the manufacturers and assigned to Arena Program Management. The exterior metal stairs that ascend the east wall were built into the parametric model in a joint effort with metal craftsman Bill Curran. The interior spiral stair and kitchen cabinets were purchased directly as kits from national fabricators. With the kitchen cabinets, the manufacturer supplied the dealer with the parametric model for designing and ordering the entire kitchen, which was assembled in situ by subcontractors working under the direction of Mark Anthony.

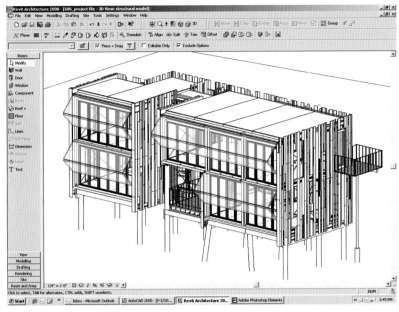

2.6

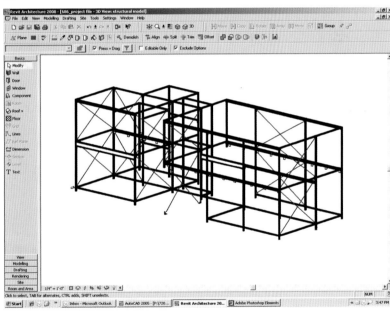

2.7

2.6
Screenshot of the fully assembled parametric
model

2.7
Screenshot of the aluminum scaffold

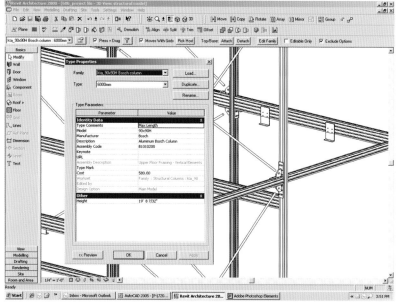

2.8

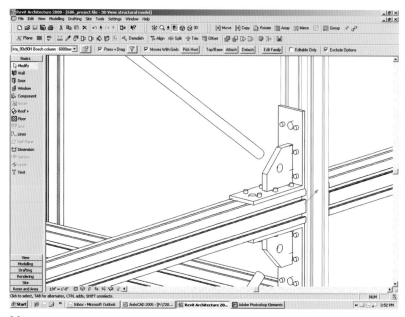

2.9

2.8
Screenshot of the parametric properties
governing an aluminum column

2.9
Screenshot of a typical scaffold joint and
diagonal bracing

As a result of being able to purchase directly from the virtual model, our entire supply chain was streamlined. Since the owner and architect of Loblolly House were a single entity, there was no transfer of risk, but one can readily imagine extending to a hybrid, supply-chain model. The advantages would be many. Long-lead-time items could be purchased and released for fabrication earlier, to ensure their availability at the correct moment in the contracted fabrication and assembly process. This information would be fully integrated into the solid model for the entirety of the design, resulting in fewer oversights and better integration. The time-consuming process of developing, submitting, and resubmitting information would be shortened. There could even be a new source of revenue for designers, as they assume some of the tasks traditionally assigned to contractors, and owners would benefit from additional savings by purchasing materials directly. The principal impediment to this shift in the supply-chain is the present legal structure, which works to isolate and assign risk between owner, designers, contractors, and subcontractors. New contractual and insurance models, often controlled by the owners, are beginning to bridge these boundaries and better integrate the parties, so that contractual terms are more consistent with the processes for managing a building information model.

2.10

2.11

2.14

2.15

2.10
Week 1: piles await installation of the collar
beam substructure

2.11
Week 3: assembly of the Bosch aluminum
frame nears completion

2.14
Week 5: cartridges and blocks for the second
level are inserted into the frame

2.15
Week 5: first layer of glazing is installed on the
west facade

2.12

2.13

2.16

2.17

2.12
Week 3: guest wing under construction

2.16
Week 6: assembly of the house nears
completion

2.13
Week 4: cartridges and blocks for the first level
are inserted into the frame

2.17
Week 9: installation of the adjustable airplane-
hangar doors

Elements, not parts

The plethora of parts that make up the contemporary building have put an end to longstanding and otherwise well focused theories of architecture. Previously, the Construction Specifications Institute organized its bewildering array of parts—numbering in the tens of thousands—into sixteen discrete divisions. More recently, this system was expanded to an astounding forty-eight divisions, but this may not be the best approach. In its place, we propose to establish fewer, highly individualized elements, such as: *site* (piles and utilities), *structure* (scaffold or frame), *floor cartridge* (wood-sheathed floor, ceiling, and roof panels with integrated structural, mechanical, and electrical systems), *block* (bathrooms enclosed in wood, with mechanical rooms and integrated fixtures, equipment, piping, wiring, and ductwork), *wall cartridge* (wood-sheathed panels with integrated windows, insulation, cement board, and vapor barrier), and *FFE elements,* including *furnishings* (movable furniture and major appliances), *fixtures* (fixed elements, such as kitchen cabinets and stairs), and *equipment* (movable elements, such as Loblolly House's folding glass wall and hangar doors). Each of these elements is first built virtually as an independent unit with parts integrated hierarchically. This manner of working allows the designer to move swiftly between individual elements, while categories for circumstantial information describe how different parts fit within the whole. At first, the modeling process focuses on specific qualities and appearances, then on joinery, and finally on integration into a full model. Working in this way, the math begins to work in *our* favor. Exponential relationships between joined elements begin to edge toward an almost linear process. The potential for fine craftsmanship re-emerges, as more focus is placed on the quality of architectural joinery.

3.1

3.1
The first pile is driven into the sandy soil to
the point of refusal, with marks at one-foot
intervals to indicate depth

Piles

When materials are anchored to the ground, they assume the potential for transformation, by circumstance, into architecture. This act of grounding—of fastening what we build to the earth—separates architecture from other acts of design. While the act of grounding is architecture's wellspring, it is also the least predictable moment in the building process. Shifting focus from the sacred role of site as origin of architecture to the profane act of implementing its attachment is where trouble often begins. Our inability to predict the outcome of our chance encounters with the earth leads most contractual arrangements for design and construction to assign to the client "absolute ownership" of the site, in the fullest sense possible. This begins with the owner commissioning topographical, utility, and soil studies and providing the results to the architects, engineers, and builders. Often it extends to the literal owning of whatever lies below, be it rock or water.

Loblolly House is grounded to the site through piles that metaphorically establish it as a house amid the trees. It is this reference, to forest as foundation, that begins the act of attachment to place. The piles are both poetic and pragmatic. They situate the house within the forest and lift it above the nontidal marshes, creating an open passageway beneath.

Compared to fabrication and assembly, which follow from the foundations, the driving of piles is extraordinarily imprecise. No matter how accurate the initial placement, after they are driven into the ground, vertical alignment, location at the first floor, and final height are varied. Two layers of collar beams are needed to align the scaffold frame with the piles below. The first collar beam layer sits on a shoulder set into the piles, tying them together. The second layer overlaps the first and brings the scaffold into alignment with the piles below. It is a gasket that allows the prefabricated elements to align with what is an inherently irregular foundation.

There is another form of connection and exchange between the house and site. While timber piles transfer structural loads to the earth, two hollow piles provide open sleeves for supplying fresh water and power and for carrying wastewater. This supplemental form of grounding connects the habitat to local resources: water and energy, two substances that are vital to life.

3.2
After five days, twenty-one piles are ready to receive the collar beam substructure

3.2

3.3

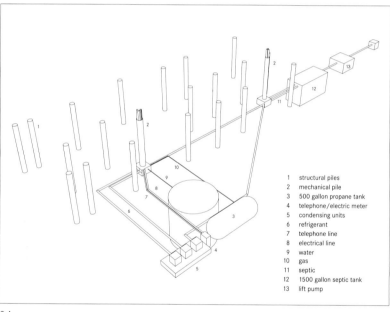

1	structural piles
2	mechanical pile
3	500 gallon propane tank
4	telephone/electric meter
5	condensing units
6	refrigerant
7	telephone line
8	electrical line
9	water
10	gas
11	septic
12	1500 gallon septic tank
13	lift pump

3.4

3.3
Parametric model of the canted piles

3.4
Utility diagram, with two hollowed piles
enclosing conduits for water and power

3.5

3.5
The collar beam substructure aligns the
foundation with the framing system

3.6

3.6
Glulam collar beams are installed on the piles, increasing the margin of accuracy for subsequent assembly

3.7
Final survey of the piles

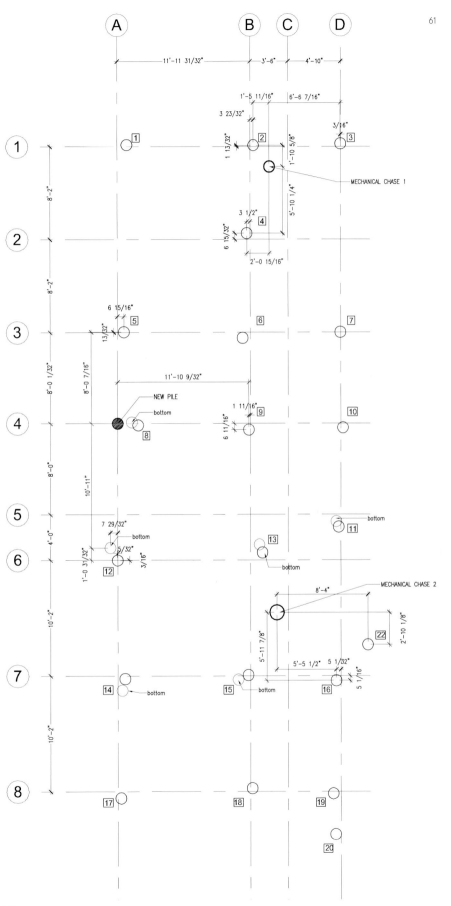

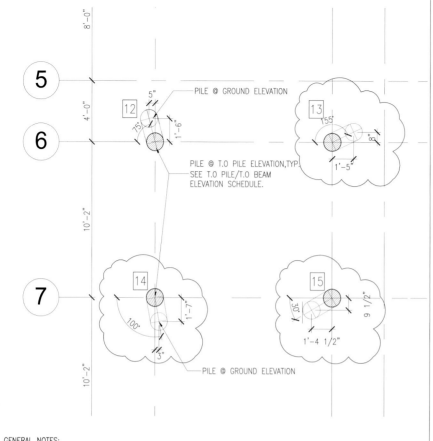

PILE @ GROUND ELEVATION

PILE @ T.O PILE ELEVATION,TYP.
SEE T.O PILE/T.O BEAM
ELEVATION SCHEDULE.

PILE @ GROUND ELEVATION

GENERAL NOTES:

1. PILES No. 12, 13, 14, 15 MUST BE DRIVEN 10 DEGREES FROM THE VERTICAL.

2. ALLOW NO LESS THAN 2'-0" AND NO MORE THAN 3'-0" OF ADDITIONAL LENGTH TO THE T.O. PILE ELEVATION GIVEN.
    AT TOP OF PILE ELEVATION:
        PILE No. 12 MUST BE CENTERED ON GRID LINES A AND 6,
        PILE No. 13 MUST BE CENTERED ON GRID LINE B AND 6,
        PILE No. 14 MUST BE CENTERED ON GRID LINE A AND 7,
        PILE No. 15 MUST BE CENTERED ON GRID LINE B AND 7.

KieranTimberlake ASSOCIATES LLP
420 NORTH 20TH STREET
PHILADELPHIA, PA 19130
V 215.922.6600 F 215.922.4680

SCALE: 1/4"=1'-0'
SHT REF: ---
DATE: 02/07/06

3.8

3.8
Survey of actual positions of canted piles

3.9

3.9
A second collar beam layer provides more
accurate alignment

Craft,
not lines

The second opportunity that the model affords is an architecture informed by materials and craft, not lines on paper. This is an unexpected turn of events, as it is often held that computers remove tactility from architecture. Actually, virtual simulation invites the opposite. To build the model, one cannot draw lines that merely represent profiles; one must build the model by thinking in terms of material and configuration. Once detailed, the assembly of each element to the next is the main focus, with joining becoming a fully simulated, three-dimensional craft. In this solid, element-based model, lines mean very little. The real stuff with which we build, materiality and method of assembly, returns to the architect's and the engineer's spheres of speculation.

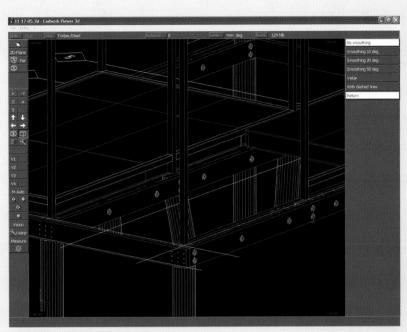

Screenshot of details embedded within the CadWorks
model developed by Bensonwood Homes

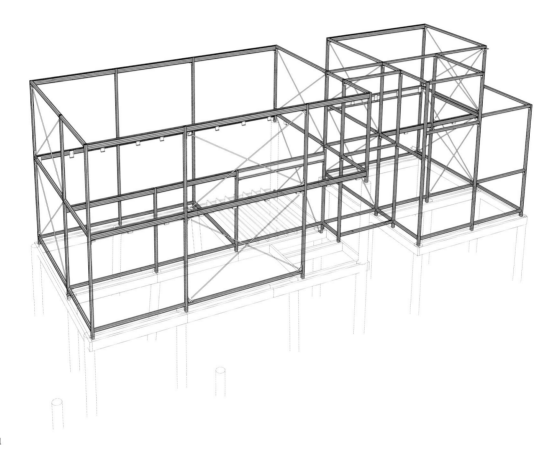

4.1

4.1
Parametric model of the aluminum scaffold and
substructure

Scaffold

There are now and have always been two basic ways of lifting and supporting architectural elements above the earth: frames and walls. Frames are capable of transferring loads from great heights through joined members that extend down to the earth. Loblolly is a frame house. It transfers its loads, applied and integral, to the pile foundations. In turn, the piles transfer loads to the earth by means of horizontal, vertical, and diagonal members that resolve themselves abstractly, as a network of vectors directing loads from horizontal beams to vertical columns and with diagonal ties providing rigidity against lateral wind forces.

Scaffolds are typically used to provide temporary, elevated work platforms along building facades or within interior spaces. At Loblolly House, the scaffold is not temporary; it forms the base internal structure. The scaffold is composed of two types of elements: extruded aluminum sections and basic connectors. The aluminum sections were selected from standard profiles from the manufacturer's catalog. The connectors are a combination of standard and custom-fabricated units. This particular scaffold system was not designed with an architectural use in mind. Ordinarily, it is used to support industrial manufacturing at a variety of scales. We found its architectural advantages to be ease of use and speed of assembly, as well as availability and flexibility. The profiles are standard extrusions and are commonly stocked, with many sections available for delivery within weeks, as opposed to months. It is a kit-of-parts system capable of producing a variety of configurations.

The primary feature of the Loblolly scaffold is the T-shaped groove located on either side of the extrusion. A source of endless innovation, this groove is uncommon in architectural structures, where the mechanism for joining steel or concrete is neither inherent nor embedded within the section. That is, joints between conventional architectural members must be constructed with considerable effort in the field, regardless of the material. In the case of steel, joints may be formed by a series of welds or by a substantial number of bolts, often coupled with intermediate connecting angles. For a concrete frame, the column-to-beam joint is reinforced by a dense network of bent bars that overlap and pass through it in all directions. In contrast, the scaffold relies on a dry joint with

4.2
The scaffold relies on a dry joint, with simple connectors that are bolted (right) instead of welded (left)

simple sleeve connections to prevent two adjoining vertical members from moving out of alignment. The source of creativity within the Loblolly scaffold is the simple T-groove, which has been exploited for as many purposes as possible. It provides the mechanism for a variety of friction connections and serves as the negative receptor for the positive T-shaped bars that fasten an array of standard and fabricated connectors to the scaffold section.

There are three kinds of connectors used to fasten beams to columns. The *primary connectors* are custom designed to transfer live and dead loads from the shear studs to the columns. The *secondary connectors* fasten vertical columns to horizontal beams. These are simple, gravity-based connectors that rely on standard triangular fittings. Bolted and held in place by friction, they restrain any minor lateral movement. A *tertiary connector* not only supports the beams and columns but also protects the entire scaffold system against major lateral forces. These diagonal ties stiffen the frame and provide resistance against forces imposed by heavy winds or an earthquake. Because the scaffold system we chose was not designed with structural loads in mind, this connector

had to be custom fabricated. Simple diagonal cables then fasten the corners at selected intervals. Floor and wall cartridges are fastened to the aluminum frame in three ways. Both cartridges use the T-groove to connect to the frame. For the typical floor cartridge, vertical Z-shaped connectors slide into the beam sections' grooved receptors and are bolted in place, supporting the floor plates like outstretched fingers. Additionally, a simple L-shaped connector has three different uses. The glass floor of the footbridge (between the two pavilions) relies on a variant L-connector. The house's roof cartridges are not hung from the scaffold beams but rest directly on top of them. In this case, a small L-shaped connector uses a T-groove to fasten the roof cartridge to the scaffold. The glass wall panels also fasten to and are supported by the scaffold frame through the L-connector.

In addition to these structural connections, the scaffold is capable of accommodating movable elements. For example, sliding doors between rooms use the scaffold as a channel.

4.3
Wall panels and floor cartridges are joined by the scaffold, at the base of the spiral staircase

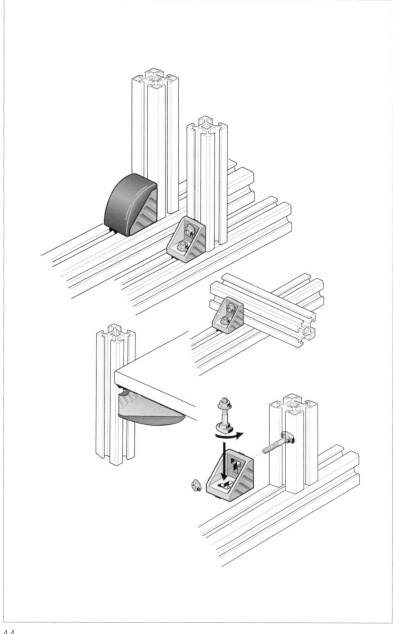

4.4

4.5

4.6

4.4
Standard connections for the Bosch aluminum framing system

4.5
Scaffold members are machined, sorted, and labeled off site in preparation for assembly

4.6
The prepackaged scaffold arrives

90-Series Profiles

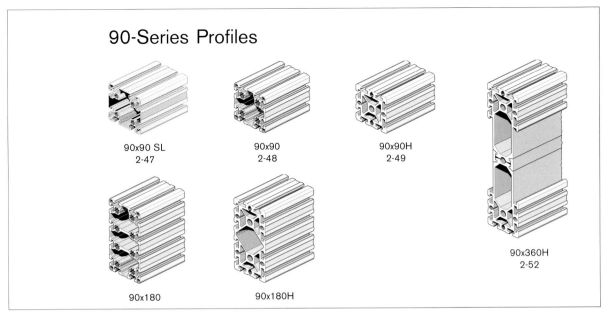

90x90 SL
2-47

90x90
2-48

90x90H
2-49

90x180

90x180H

90x360H
2-52

4.7

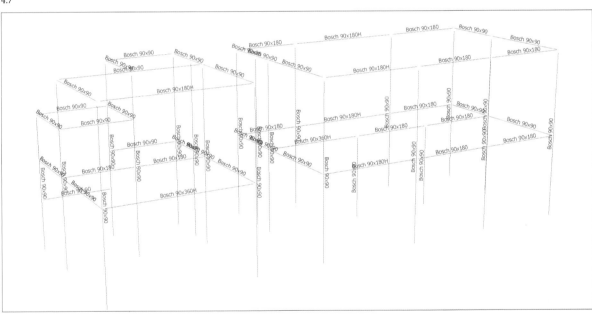

4.8

4.7
Profiles of the Bosch aluminum members,
depicting the T-groove receptor

4.8
Diagram of the sizes required for framing

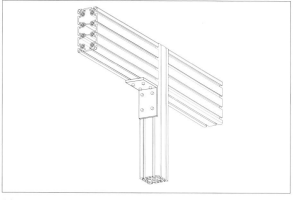

4.9

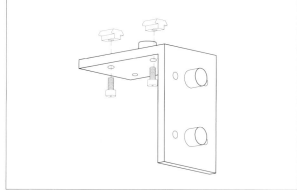

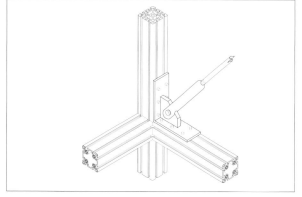

4.10

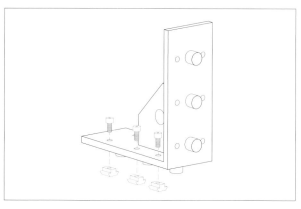

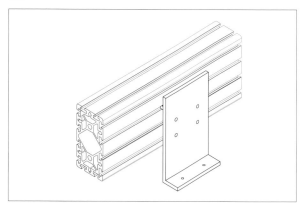

4.11

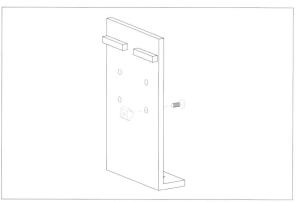

4.9
Custom fabricated L-shaped connector

4.10
Custom fabricated diagonal bracing

4.11
Custom fabricated Z-shaped connector

4.12
Structural connections at the entrance to the glass footbridge

4.13

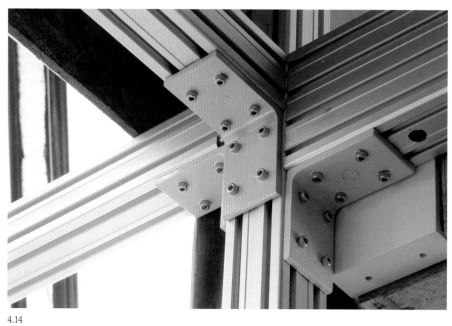

4.14

4.13
The aluminum was predrilled and fitted with
connectors off site

4.14
L-shaped column-to-beam connectors

4.15

4.16

4.15
Z-shaped connectors that suspend the floor
cartridges

4.16
Bosch aluminum frame prior to the installation
of cartridges

4.17

4.18

4.17
On-site assembly of column-to-beam
connectors and diagonal bracing

4.18
Aluminum connection with precut glulam
beams

4.19
Finished view of the scaffold, floor, and wall
cartridge connections

4.20

4.20
By day three of assembly, the aluminum
scaffold is ready to receive the blocks and
cartridges

4.21
Finished view of the glass footbridge and spiral
stair separating the guest wing from the main
house

Assembly,
not construction

Loblolly House was assembled, not constructed. This distinction is present on several levels. Assembly is fast; construction takes much longer. Assembly can be performed with rudimentary skill and just a few simple tools. Construction, on the other hand, is complex and often requires considerable skill, training, and specialized tools and equipment. Assembly depends on factory-controlled cutting, prefitting, drilling, and jigging; it dictates field fabrication methods and fittings; and it can be completed with the aid of written directions. For the most part, construction is directed by unwritten knowledge passed along through formal training and apprenticeship. This distinction is of further relevance when comparing frames to scaffolds. Frames are constructed; scaffolds are assembled. Frames require skill, knowledge, and specialized equipment. Scaffolds require only some directions and a wrench. The individual members are light, can be handled for swift erection using only a fastener, and they can be completed in minutes. In

this sense, the scaffold is closer conceptually to an
erector set. Unlike most structural frames, it is readily
reversible and can be disassembled as quickly, or
more quickly, than it can be assembled. It does not
require a demolition crew, nor do the materials
need to be destroyed in the process. A scaffold can be
unbolted with a wrench and is fully recyclable.

Through the agency of the scaffold, one can begin to
imagine a new market based on relocation instead
of demolition. Often times, real estate cycles force the
market to abandon buildings long before their
constituent materials have carried out their life cycles.
The scaffold represents the beginning of an idea
about architecture's structured engagement with site
and our critical obligation to downcycling. The scaffold
reinterprets structure. It is a fulcrum of possibilities
for structuring space and, at the same time, provides
an open network for connection, extension,
disengagement, and relocation.

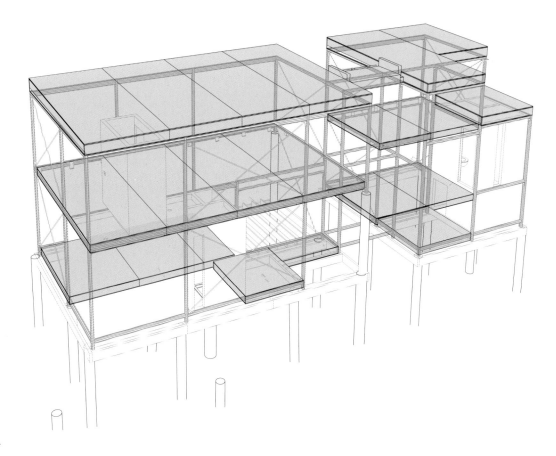

5.1

5.1
Parametric model of floor and roof cartridges

Cartridge

All cartridges have one feature in common: a shell that contains and protects a valuable working core. Both the shell and the core may assume many forms. They may have plastic casings loaded with ink, tape, or film. They can be organized for mass distribution through a printer or tape player, or they may consist of metal casings loaded with explosives organized for lethal distribution. The shell of a cartridge not only protects its fragile cargo but internally organizes that cargo for intelligent, on-demand delivery. The cartridge shell, however, is more than just a simple container. It may be shaped and formed for specific aerodynamic or structural purposes, as with a bullet; or it may have internal compartments, guides, and rollers, as in a tape cartridge. The core is typically made of material of a higher, more intelligent order than what might be found in a simple container. This is what makes *cartridge* an ideal term for an element-based architecture.

For the most part each of the architectural elements that compose Loblolly House perform a single function. Structural elements provide support. Sheeting materials sometimes provide support but more often just enclose. Conduits, pipes, and ducts channel electricity, water, and air, respectively. While theory and practice tend to codify separation, the cartridge concept does not. It supports the functional integration of several systems in a prefabricated, ready-to-install component assembly. As with a cassette tape, the Loblolly cartridge is an intelligent, multivalent container for the distribution of systems.

Within the house, the cartridge shell performs three basic functions. First, it handles live loads imposed by people, furnishings, and inclement weather, as well as dead structural loads from its own weight. The shell is composed of lumber ribs and plywood sheathing, and its loads are transferred to the scaffold. Second, the sheathing protects and contains the fragile and intelligent conduit elements for water, air, and electricity. Water passing through built-in plastic piping provides radiant heat for the entire house, carries hot and cold water to faucets and appliances, and supports the distribution of wastewater. Flexible microducts distribute conditioned air and provide ventilation to the cartridges. Also, built-in electrical conduits power light fixtures and ceiling fans.

One way to conceptualize the wall cartridge is to think of it as a packaging system composed of skin and a

5.2
Like an audio cassette, a cartridge is a container designed to protect a valuable working core

core. A skeletal frame organizes the core materials that support the house's principle functions and provide varying degrees of separation from the elements of nature. The elements we seek shelter from are the same now as they have always been: water, air, and sun. The primary purpose of architecture is to protect us from water, to temper the air around us, and to protect us from the sun. The objective is not to separate us completely from these elements, as an envelope would, but to filter and manage the forces of nature and to sustain and support the comfort of the inhabitants. Toward this end, the outer skin of the Loblolly cartridge is sheathed in an open-joint cedar rainscreen. The screen is both aesthetic and pragmatic. It provides a visual scrim that mimics the loblolly forest and reinforces the home's relationship to site. By filtering rain and solar radiation, it protects the underlying cement boards and gives the interior walls an extra layer of protection. Essentially, the outer skin functions as the home's first line of defense.

Between the inner and outer skins of the cartridge, studs structurally frame and support the exterior and interior panels and bring these elements into alignment.

In Loblolly House, these studs are necessary. They make the inner and outer skins rigid, but more importantly, they function as spacers. They provide a cavity that, enhanced with low-conducting materials, insulates inside from outside and filters and controls the transfer of air. When filled with insulation, this cavity becomes a core and also functions as a cartridge. Vapor barriers (filters that line the insulated core) allow moist air to pass through the walls. Together with the insulation, these barriers create comfortable interior environments.

The wall cartridge provides one more type of filter: the window, which transmits light, frames views, and, if operable, allows for the passage of air. With Loblolly House, the prefabricated window units were built into cartridges off-site. These units, which measure the full height of the wall and have built-in, roll-up screens, were delivered to the fabricator and integrated into the cartridges as they were assembled.

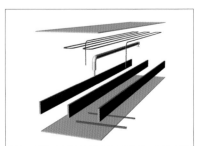

5.3
Diagram of a typical floor cartridge, embedded with structural members, radiant heating, microducts, electrical conduits, and exterior sheathing

5.3

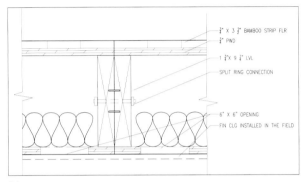

5.4

¾" X 3 ½" BAMBOO STRIP FLR
¾" PWD

1 ¾" X 9 ¼" LVL

SPLIT RING CONNECTION

6" X 6" OPENING
FIN CLG INSTALLED IN THE FIELD

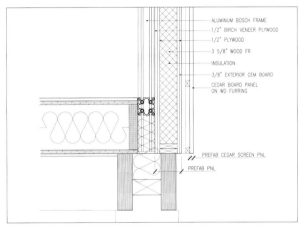

5.5

ALUMINUM BOSCH FRAME
1/2" BIRCH VENEER PLYWOOD
1/2" PLYWOOD
3 5/8" WOOD FR
INSULATION
3/8" EXTERIOR CEM BOARD
CEDAR BOARD PANEL
ON WD FURRING

PREFAB CEDAR SCREEN PNL
PREFAB PNL

5.6

5.7

5.4
Diagram of the connection between floor
cartridges

5.5
Diagram of the intersection between the facade
and floor cartridges

5.6
Shop installation of tubes for radiant heating

5.7
Floor cartridges prior to the addition of
electrical conduits and insulation

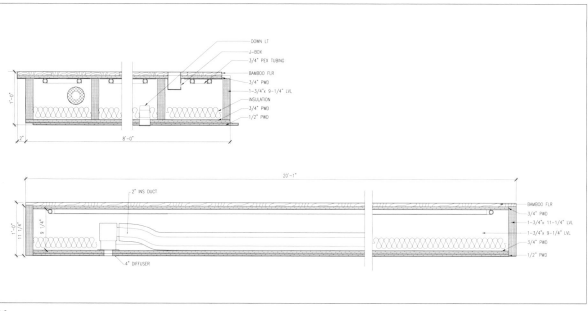

DOWN LT
J-BOX
3/4" PEX TUBING
BAMBOO FLR
3/4" PWD
1-3/4"x 9-1/4" LVL
INSULATION
3/4" PWD
1/2" PWD

1'-0"
2"
8'-0"

2" INS DUCT
BAMBOO FLR
3/4" PWD
1-3/4"x 11-1/4" LVL
1-3/4"x 9-1/4" LVL
3/4" PWD
1/2" PWD

20'-1"

1'-0 1/4"
11 1/4"
9 1/4"
4" DIFFUSER

5.8

5.8
Section diagram of a standard floor cartridge

5.9

5.10

5.11

5.9 and 5.10
Floor cartridges are lifted by crane and inserted
into the frame

5.11
Roof and second-level floor cartridges are
"hung" from the scaffold

5.12

5.12
As-built plan of floor cartridges

5.13

5.13
View of the master bedroom and bathroom
module under construction

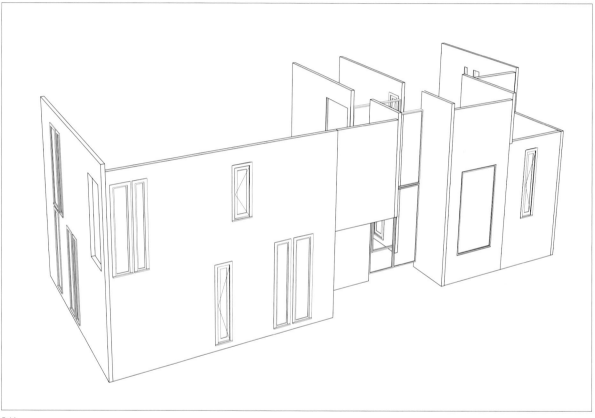

5.14

5.14
Parametric model of wall cartridges

5.15

5.17

5.16

5.18

5.15
The guest wing almost fully sheathed

5.16
A wall cartridge is lowered into place

5.17
A tarp is placed over the guest wing

5.18
A wall cartridge is bolted in place

5.19

5.19
Installation detail, prior to the attachment of
the cedar rainscreen and interior finishes

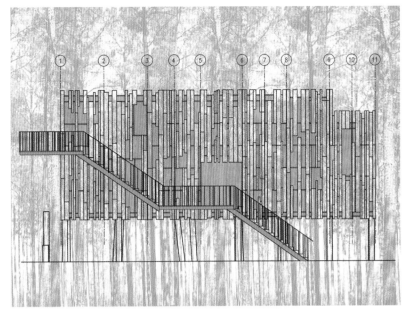

5.20

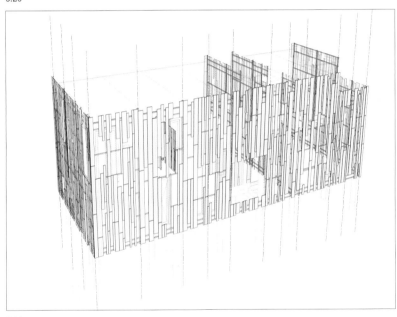

5.21

5.20
The pattern of the cedar rainscreen was
composed over a photograph of the loblolly
forest

5.21
Parametric model of cedar rainscreen and
underlying structural elements

5.22

5.24

5.23

5.25

5.22
Prefabricated cedar rainscreen ready for installation

5.23
The rainscreen is attached to the house in segments

5.24
A panel is lifted in place

5.25
Positioning and bolting the panel

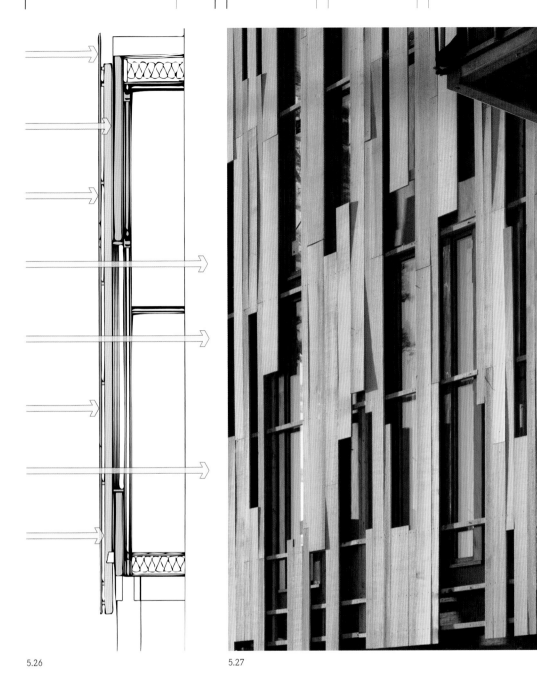

5.26

5.27

5.26
Section of the bilayer facade

5.27
Overlapping cedar boards act as a filter for
rain, wind, and solar radiation

Overleaf:
5.28
On-site installation of prefabricated steel stairs

5.29

5.29
Orange glass illuminates the house's core,
emphasizing the sun's role in the fusion of
nature and architecture

5.30

5.30
The platform entry to the second level projects
like an osprey nest

Quilting,
not weaving

Dimensional certainty is a direct product of the parametric model. Each element is assembled into a geometric whole that must be "closed in all directions." That is, each element links to the next until they form a cohesive whole. If a single dimension or set of dimensions is incorrect, either too short or long, then the model discloses a "failure to close," inviting the modelmaker to correct the problem. Though it may not seem like a paradigm-shifting advance, the ramifications of this tool are substantial, as compared to the dimensional uncertainty that now prevails. In current practice, a building is woven together as a series of systems. We measure as we go, ensuring the fit of each successive element. In contrast, the parametric model embeds geometric and dimensional certainty within it, as opposed to unearthing these details during construction. Through the agency of this digital tool, we can become confident quilters, rather than tentative weavers. We can fabricate multiple elements simultaneously and assemble them on-site. We no longer have to wait for a prior element to arrive to proceed with the fabrication of interdependent systems. Our modern forefathers did not possess these powerful parametric tools. The uncertainty of prior measurements compromised their efforts at off-site fabrication. Without dimensional certainty, tolerances expand and quality suffers; or, one simply waits until prior work is in place, slowing down the process and losing the advantages of factory-based production processes.

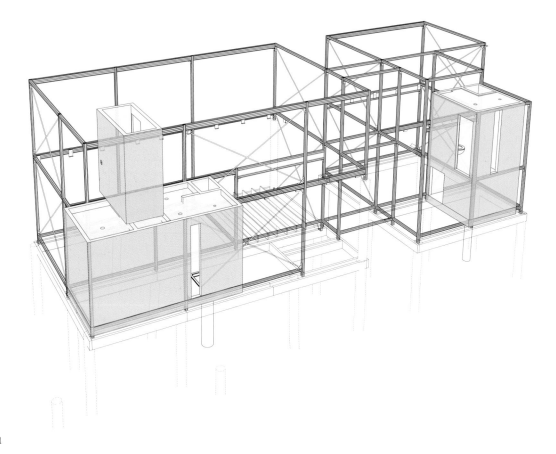

6.1

6.1
Parametric model of mechanical, electrical, and
plumbing blocks within the scaffold

Block

Terms define how we think and how we make. As individual elements abstracted from context, block and module are quite similar. Each encloses space, a three-dimensional volume replete with building systems and internal and external finishes, and both are usually fabricated in their entirety in an off-site factory or shop. Where they differ is in their strategic aggregation. In architectural terms, *module* implies a strategy of expansion. Modular architecture results from the organization of repetitive modules. Each module must have an integrated internal structure that, in combination with other modules, forms the superstructure of a building. Modular strategies often depend on shipping the largest elements possible within certain limitations, such as highway clearance or other transport requirements.

In contrast to module, the term *block* implies a surgical tactic. It is strategic and should be limited to a few, figural insertions within the scaffold field. Each block is selected for maximum constructive impact. Because blocks are often the largest and heaviest elements of the new architecture, they are best used sparingly. Minimizing the shipment of air is an important constraint for architectural optimization. Scaffold and cartridge are the best tactics for forming large, open spaces, as they can be shipped flat and stacked without air. The block, however, is best deployed within the scaffold for system-intensive spaces.

Loblolly House has three system-intensive blocks. First, a combined bathroom, closet, and mechanical room adjoins the master bedroom. Second, the guest bathroom stacks above a half-level-high mechanical room. Third, a mechanical room and closet adjoin the kitchen. Compared to other spaces, bathrooms typically require that a greater number of trades spend more time in small areas. There are several fixtures to be plumbed, including sinks, toilet, and shower. Also integral to the bathroom are ventilation fans and ducts, heating and cooling distribution and piping, electrical outlets, and light fixtures. The finishes are intensive and wet, with tile and stone the usual materials of choice, and there are many accessories. The sequencing of so many trades in such a small space makes these rooms among the longest and most troubling critical paths in construction. Because they are relatively small and can be shipped without special permits, the bathroom is the ideal candidate for factory-built or shop-fabricated blocks.

Blocks are the organs of Loblolly House. They contain mechanical and electrical manifolds that organize and manage all incoming and outgoing utility connections. The manifold idea is common for electricity but less so for mechanical systems. Loblolly's manifolds direct the distribution of cold water, hot water for faucets, and water for radiant heating. These systems are distributed through the cartridges, using long leads for connections running laterally across the field-installed mechanical spine and culminating at the manifolds in the mechanical blocks. The flexible tubing includes: a plastic pipe for water, an insulated wire for electric, and ductwork for air (with dry-friction and clamp connections). The appropriate distribution pipe, wire, or duct is simply quick-coupled onto the matching joint manifold, with no hot connections formed by soldering or otherwise fusing pipe, wire, or ductwork.

6.2

6.2
The master-bath block under construction in
the fabrication shop

6.3

6.4

6.5

6.3
The interior of the mechanical block

6.4
Mechanical and electrical manifolds for
managing all incoming and outgoing utility
connections

6.5
A combination bath and mechanical block is
lowered into place

6.6
Second-level floor cartridges are installed after
the first-level blocks

Schedules,
not myths

Inherent in parametric modeling is the ability to develop an integrated visual schedule, complete with supply-chain information for managing the arrival of elements and materials on site. Our entire team—representing design, fabrication, and assembly—modeled the project element by element, testing different strategies, sequences, and manpower scenarios, and tracking their associated time durations. We developed a visual schedule for nearly the entire construction process (except the piles and collar beam foundation). At first, our proposed schedule proved too optimistic, owing largely to the inexperience of the entire team with the methods of assembly. Initially, we hoped to erect the house in two weeks, but eventually we settled on a three-to-four-week construction duration. Even this scenario, however, didn't allow for adequate time to deal with the site's unpredictable conditions: at the slightest chance of rain, work had to be covered; wind became a significant problem when crane-lifting large but relatively light panels; and the fragile site became particularly difficult to work with when wet. We also didn't take into account a late-emerging scheduling problem in the factory that prevented the rainscreen assemblies from being attached to wall cartridges off-site. As a result, Bensonwood's site time (collar beams notwithstanding) extended to approximately six weeks. Like the detailing of the design itself, the scheduling exercise could have benefited from additional iterative, large-screen criticisms of the virtual model by all collaborators. Nevertheless, our effort revealed that current approaches, including the abstract bar chart and critical path method, could become obsolete.

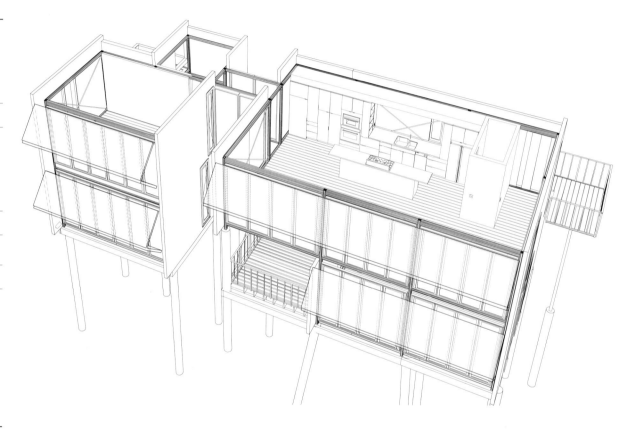

7.1

7.1
Parametric model of the kitchen fixtures,
finishes, and bamboo floors

FFE

FIXTURES

Fixtures make daily life possible within our architecture. They are among the things we interact with most as we go about our daily routines. Through a well thought-out selection process, architects participate actively in contemporary, economic, and cultural life. Still, the choosing of fixtures remains an underrated art form. As designers, we seek to impress our hands and minds upon each and every architectural detail, but the careful art of selection provokes an engagement whereby found artifacts are placed, by circumstance, within our architecture. Sometimes the selection of fixtures can seem like an all-or-nothing act, but more often, the fixtures we specify are customizable and come with a preselected array of options.

The two main fixtures in the Loblolly House are a kitchen for preparing food and staircases for moving vertically through the interior and exterior. Generally, they are either fastened to the scaffold or secured to the cartridge. Unlike many of the house's elements, however, fixtures typically arrive as prefabricated kits, and they can be removed and replaced with relative ease. For example, the interior spiral staircase and the cascading exterior stair, both considered fixtures, arrived preassembled and were attached on site. The spiral stair was delivered as a dense package with a pole and individual treads that interlock in ascending order to form a spine. The custom-fabricated exterior stair arrived in three sections with built-in railings, and we simply posted it on top of the piles.

The kitchen industry has become considerably adept at mass customizing fixtures with a range of parts. Quite a few brand name fabricators carry extensive lines of cabinetry with various forms, styles, profiles, and levels of quality. Like the automotive industry, kitchen fabricators have also developed sub-brands. Selecting from hundreds of modules, box types, interior fittings, accessories, and hardware, the customer chooses the brand and builds the design virtually. Element by element, profiles are selected and materials for drawer fronts and cabinet doors are applied to the design. Module types are substituted back and forth; elements are selected, rejected, and recombined; and new iterations are viewed in real time. The costs associated with each element are then identified

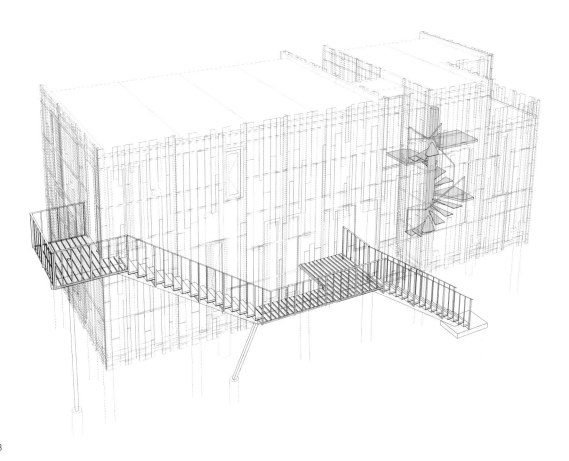

7.3

7.2
Exterior steel staricase fabricated by off-site
metalworker Bill Curran

7.3
Parametric model of exterior stairs and interior
spiral staircase

and totaled in an integrated building information model. (BIM technology has been operative in the cabinet industry for several years.) The fully integrated model —representing design through selection and including implications of cost and schedule—prefigures the technological reality that Loblolly House aspires to. The elements are fabricated directly from data captured in the model and delivered at a fixed price and schedule.

FURNISHINGS

Beyond the selection of finish materials and colors, the furnishings at Loblolly were not custom designed. Initially, we thought that the furnishings should extend the aesthetic of the house and therefore be made of wood and metal. With the intervention of Marguerite Rodgers as interior design consultants, the notion of a fixed palette gradually gave way to a matrix based on four principles derived from the house's dominant architectural features: fusing materials with elements of the site, such as the native cordgrass and pines; integrating prefabricated furnishings of an earlier generation of high modernists; selecting affordable low-modern furnishings

from the 1960s onward; and celebrating the fine joinery of historic Asian furnishings while also considering design for disassembly. As with the house's architectural elements, we hoped the furnishings would convey our reverence for the art of selection and, in doing so, elevate the supply chain to an act of design. Rather than draw from a narrow palette, we undertook the more complex path of selecting pieces one by one, which demanded a diverse supply chain with numerous vendors at the helm of the interior designer.

The selection process evolved into a consideration of the house's overall context, including its reverence for the surrounding environment, its manner of production, and our own aspirations for affordability. Just as the materials were selected with renewable resources in mind, so were many of the furnishings. The carpets, which resemble woven cordgrass, rest on top of green bamboo floors. Both layers evoke the site's ground plane. The vintage dining table designed by John Widdicomb—with staggered planks of differing grains—further extends the forest metaphor. Upholstery for the living room couch features vertically striated lines of green, brown, and

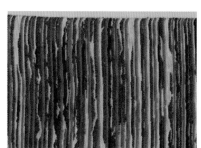

7.4
Carpet for the living room, resembling woven cordgrass

7.5
Upholstery for the living room, with striations of green, brown, and yellow

7.4   7.5

7.6

7.6
Main living and dining area

7.7

7.7
Master bedroom, with adjustable west facade
in the open position

yellow. Two Hans Wegner–designed chairs were chosen, not only for their beautiful profiles but also for their bentwood structure and woven cane seats. An ancient material, cane is as renewable today as it was thousands of years ago, and it exists naturally on the site.

The furnishings we've selected also forge connections to the design, fabrication, and assembly of the house. Our off-site fabrication agenda is not new; it is a recurring modernist concern that dates from the turn of the twentieth century. Nearly every high-modern architect of relevance took a turn at solving the ongoing demand for prefabricated mass housing. This history provides the third context for the selection of furnishings. Swivel lounge chairs in the living room pay homage to Charles and Ray Eames, who, in many ways, are Loblolly House's intellectual predecessors. In their own home, ordinary off-the-shelf elements were transformed into works of art. They molded plywood into the classic shape known today as the Eames Chair, two of which have been placed on either side of the sofa. A molded plastic chair in one of the bedrooms is also of their design.

Perhaps more so than any high modernist, Le Corbusier confronted the mass-housing dilemma head-on. He considered it the architect's obligation to provide quality housing at low cost. For him, it was fundamental to the profession, and he revisited the challenge throughout his career. The photographs of cars, ships, and airplanes in *Towards a New Architecture* included their mode of assembly in factories. To generations of architects and builders, these images were a call to action. The early twentieth century, however, was not equipped with the kinds of information management tools and labor structures that we have at our disposal today. To acknowledge Le Corbusier's clarion, we've placed his LC1 chair in one of the bedrooms. Other high-modernist objects by designers such as Harry Bertoia have been placed for their singular appropriateness within the context of the house.

The low-modern tradition of the 1960s and '70s–variously called *art moderne* or *vintage modern*–followed the lead of the high-modern classics. Designed for mass consumption, such furnishings have historically been marketed throughout Scandinavia, Europe, and the

7.8
LC1 Chair, Le Corbusier, architect

7.8

United States. For example, turned wooden lamps, serving trays, and the dining room table all stem from this genre. In the guest bedrooms, the end tables, blanket chests, and beds celebrate this tradition of affordable modernism, as do the Italian Glo-Ball lamps designed by Jasper Morrison, which anchor both sides of the great room.

The final context for the furnishings is derived from non-Western cultures, specifically Japanese and Chinese furnishings of the late nineteenth and early twentieth centuries. Cultural objects from these time periods were a generative source of design for many Western architects working in the early twentieth century. The abstraction of Japanese and Chinese wood detailing and joinery made its way into the work of numerous early modern architects in the United States, such as Greene and Greene and Frank Lloyd Wright. Their architecture was one of exposed structure that, especially in the case of temples, was designed with disassembly in mind. Many of Loblolly's furnishings celebrate these traditions. Among the most beautiful and useful is a Japanese mingei stool sculpted out of a single log. A notch carved

several inches below the top provides a finger hole for lifting the stool. The natural tendency of the log to split as it dries is dealt with in a simple and matter-of-fact way, through the placement of structural patches in the form of wooden butterfly connectors.

In place of closets, Chinese wardrobes crafted out of light-colored wood provide storage in the bedrooms. Also of Chinese origin, wood and metal tables painted red and green serve as buffets in the dining room and provide a colored counterpoint to the birch plywood details. A black-lacquered library cabinet in the form of a small staircase offers a place for books and storage at the first-level entry. As a result of these diverse selections, we were able to create a visually rich palette, and each furnishing is, in its own way, in conversation with the architecture.

7.9

7.9
Dining room with vintage table designed by
John Widdicomb

7.11

7.10
View from guest wing through bamboo garden

7.11
Covered porch adjoining the master bedroom

Overleaf:
7.12
Exterior, west facade with hangar doors fully open

EQUIPMENT

We define *equipment* as machinery capable of purposefully adjusting its performance. Such structures are becoming increasingly important elements within our architecture, helping us to tune our habitats to specific environmental conditions. Historically, our designed responses to the environment have been structured around averages of temperature, daylight, wind, precipitation, and other circumstances. Extreme conditions are usually dealt with by elimination, through the use of membranes that curtail them altogether. While average environmental conditions provide the basis for much of our design, significant advantages can be had by considering extreme conditions. Equipment has the potential to extend that realm to include precise circumstances of time, season, and place.

Within Loblolly House, the west facade overlooking the Chesapeake Bay is the piece of equipment that allows for rapid adjustment to extreme exposure. Exterior walls facing north, south, and east are fixed cartridges and contain just a few windows, several of them operable. The degree of exposure from the west, however, introduces the need for a sophisticated filtration system to temper local conditions. The adjustable facade—consisting of polycarbonate-clad airplane hangar doors—allows for three levels of closure against wind, water, and solar gain. The translucent doors serve two purposes: they act as a bifolding awning system, shielding against extreme angles of the sun, or they can be kept high and flat, providing shade when the sun is high in the sky. When the house is unoccupied during the late fall and winter seasons, the hangar doors can be fully closed for storm protection. The doors trap solar heat in an air pocket between the two glazing systems, creating a blanket of warmth during the day and mitigating heat loss during colder weather. The double-skin facade is an environmental machine, allowing the internal climate to adapt across extremes from completely open to fully secure. Coupled with automated insect screens, they turn the west-facing rooms into open interior porches with vistas toward the bay that not only provide expansive views but ample cross-ventilation from prevailing water-to-land breezes.

Natural ventilation is the predominant environmental mode during the fall, spring, and summer months.

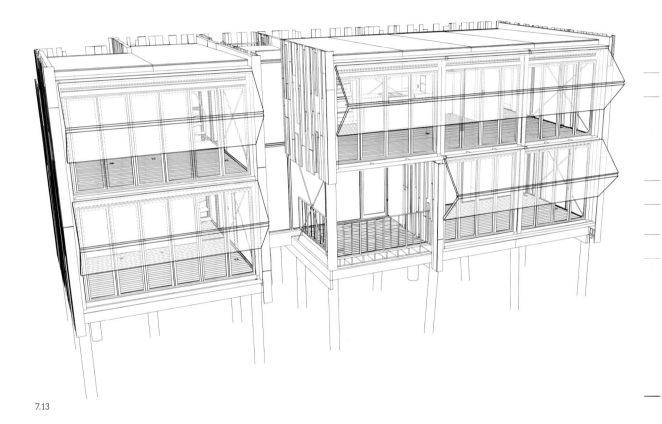

7.13

7.13
Parametric model of bifolding
hangar doors

7.14

7.14
Twilight view, with hangar doors
under construction

7.15

7.15
Translucent polycarbonate doors
tuned to the afternoon sun

Although the house is equipped with a backup air-conditioning system, our objective was to uninvent this technology. In fact, we relied on air-conditioning only three times during the first summer. Instead, we took advantage of basic principles of ventilation to manipulate natural pressure differentials. Seasonal temperature differences generate steady water-to-land breezes, particularly in the evenings. Because there are only a few operable windows and doors on the east facade, the house becomes an oversized fan chamber when the adjustable facade is completely open. Pressure generated by large volumes of air—entering from the west and seeking to leave through small apertures to the east—produces interior differentials, even when winds are slight. In all but the most humid conditions, air circulating through the house cools the spaces and its occupants. The accordion-style doors can be tuned to an infinite number of positions based on external conditions, admitting more or less air, as desired. Similarly, windows and doors on the east wall can be left open, partially open, or closed to control the wind's speed as it enters and exits. Loblolly House may be rooted to the ground, but, in some sense, it functions like a great sailboat. There is joy in manipulating the house's relationship to the natural world. Throughout the day, inhabitants are keenly aware of what is going on outside and revel in their newfound ability to work with, rather than against, the natural world.

Nowadays, we build our architecture and hope that everything works as designed. Monitoring and fine-tuning the performance of building systems rarely happen on an ongoing basis. Our architecture is not viewed as a lifelong obligation. But with the increasing demand for high-performance buildings, this is beginning to change. For a small percentage of LEED-certified buildings, post-occupancy commissioning is now a requirement. Commissioning agents, building engineers, and subcontractors work together to ensure that the performance requirements specified by the designer are actually met. Their objective is to get the architecture to perform as intended but never to have it perform *better* than intended. Furthermore, within the existing process, there is little opportunity to reflect on how we might do things better the next time around.

7.16
The bifolding doors in the awning position

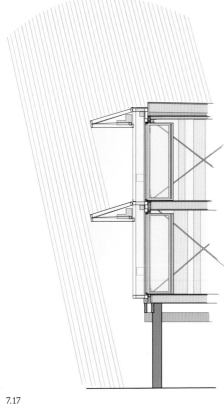

7.17

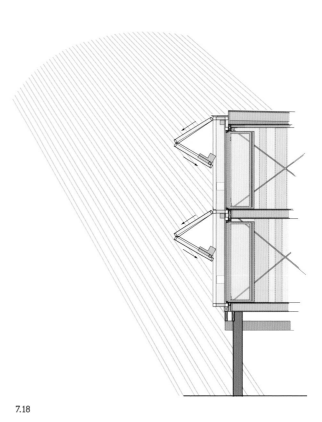

7.18

7.17
At midday, with bifolding doors in the high
position to deflect the sun's rays

7.18
In the late afternoon, with bifolding doors in the
semiopen position to filter incoming light

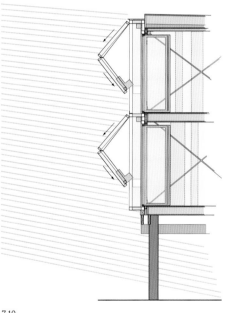

7.19

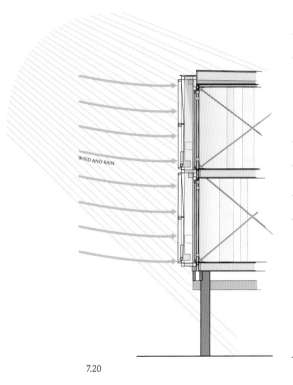

WIND AND RAIN

7.20

7.19
During the early evening, with bifolding doors
lowered to filter the sun's extreme angle

7.20
In the closed position, the bifolding doors
provide storm protection and trap solar heat in
an air pocket between the two glazing systems

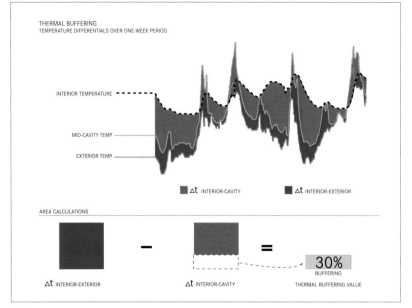

7.21

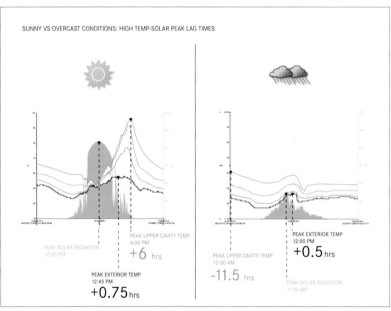

7.22

7.21
Postoccupancy monitoring of the adjustable
facade, test results

7.22
Results for post-peak solar radiation

At Loblolly House, we undertook an effort to monitor the performance of the west wall for two reasons: to see how variable wind and temperature conditions would impact the glazing and to compare performance to actual data. With each season, we'll be recording actual temperatures under different environmental conditions, with the doors in a range of positions. Carefully positioned sensors measure air temperatures outside, within the double-glazed window cavity, on exterior and interior glazed surfaces, and inside the rooms. There were two sets of sensors, one for the upper room (located at the top of the cavity) and one for the lower. We also installed motion sensors to track the positions of the hangar doors and roof sensors to measure the degree of general radiance.

Data compiled during the first winter confirmed several of our intuitions. During sunny winter afternoons—with the exterior polycarbonate doors closed—air inside the cavity got warmer. The monitors showed that warming within the cavity amounted to 30 percent of the difference between desired outside and inside air temperatures. We were also surprised to observe that the temperature differential continued for several hours into the evening before dissipating, significantly lowering heating loads at a time when we were still awake and active in the house. Further analysis of the data suggested that additional design modifications could enhance the performance of the west facade. We noticed that warm air rises to the top of the two-story cavity, providing more thermal benefit to the upper level. Placing an insulating board beneath the grating created a double-stack effect for warming both floors equally. In addition, ducts activated by thermal-coupled dampers will be installed to pull warm air generated by the afternoon sun through the floor cartridges and into the rooms. This will extend the solar warming benefits well into the afternoon and evening.

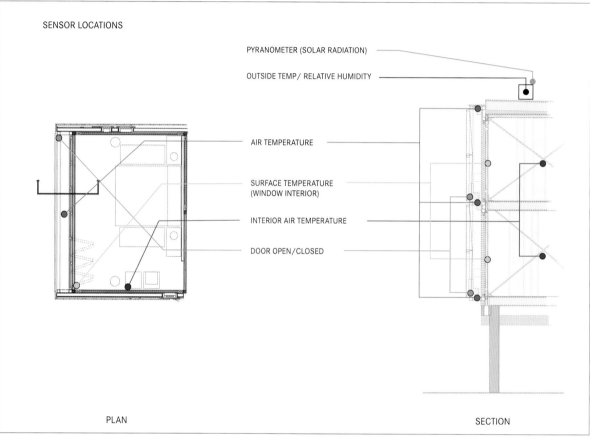

SENSOR LOCATIONS

PYRANOMETER (SOLAR RADIATION)

OUTSIDE TEMP/ RELATIVE HUMIDITY

AIR TEMPERATURE

SURFACE TEMPERATURE
(WINDOW INTERIOR)

INTERIOR AIR TEMPERATURE

DOOR OPEN/CLOSED

PLAN

SECTION

7.23

7.23
Location of sensors for postoccupancy testing

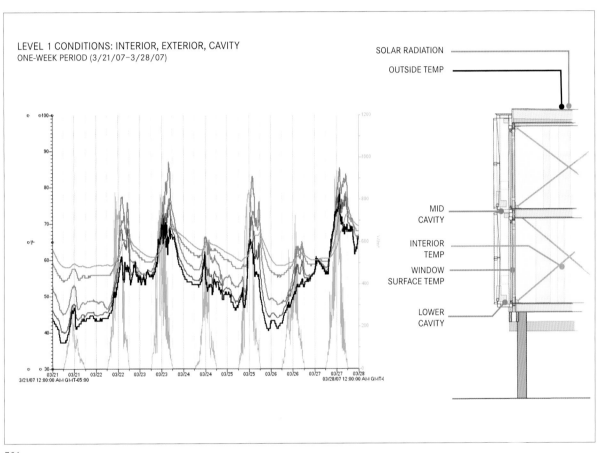

LEVEL 1 CONDITIONS: INTERIOR, EXTERIOR, CAVITY
ONE-WEEK PERIOD (3/21/07–3/28/07)

SOLAR RADIATION

OUTSIDE TEMP

MID
CAVITY

INTERIOR
TEMP

WINDOW
SURFACE TEMP

LOWER
CAVITY

7.24

7.24
Postoccupancy temperature variations in the
upper and lower cavities of the double-glazed
facade and interior, over a one-week period

7.25

7.26

7.25 and 7.26
Guest bedroom with adjustable facade in the
open (top) and closed (bottom) positions

7.27

7.27
Guest bedroom, with bifolding hangar doors
and sliding interior doors both semiopen

Overleaf:
7.28
Twilight view, with inner and outer facades
tuned to evening conditions

Disassembly,
not demolition

As architects, we focus on making, but we should also take responsibility for undoing the things we have made. What if we were to consider not only the origins but the eventual conclusions of our designs? This last step in the supply-chain is one that most architects and builders choose to ignore. In many cultures, especially Western ones, it is widely accepted that most buildings will survive well beyond the average person's life span. With proper care *some* buildings can endure for centuries, but these are the exceptions. It is estimated that the average American house will last forty years, but the life cycles of its constituent materials and assemblies are capable of extending well beyond that duration. Though a sizable market for architectural salvage, reclaimed materials, and recycled fixtures has emerged, a vast amount of embodied energy continues to be left behind. Instead, we should conceive our architecture in the same way that manufacturers conceive cars, as collections of used parts that remain ripe for reconditioning and reuse. The greatest impediment we face in developing a comprehensive used-parts industry, however, lies in the way we design and construct. First, we do not build with disassembly in mind. To take apart a concrete frame, we pulverize it. To disassemble a welded steel frame, we cut or torch it. A traditional platform-framed house contains so many nails that the lumber is virtually unsalvageable. Beyond the damage imposed by irreversible fasteners, many parts exist as singular elements, not as integrated components. Recycling and reconditioning tens of thousands of disaggregated parts requires so much labor that, at the moment, there is no viable, economic model for implementing a used-parts market. But if an element-based housing industry were to emerge, the cost, embodied energy, and long-term environmental footprint of our architecture would improve considerably.

*Proto*types

In his introduction to this book Michael Stacey suggests that if Loblolly House were to remain a prototype, it will have failed. That is, for a prefabricated house to truly succeed, it must be capable of being adapted to the general housing market. We disagree. While it is true that the landscape of modernism has seen countless prefabricated one-offs, the problem lies not with architects' good intentions—to implement an affordable prefab house for the masses—but with the concept of *prototype*, as it is applied. As we see it, there is too much *type* and not enough *proto*. Type suggests something ultimately recognizable, having attained a status of its own. Proto implies origins and the process of arriving at a potential solution. While we are all for *proto*, we have reservations about *type* and feel that there is no such final solution; there are only evolving sets of elements that help us make better decisions. Loblolly House represents a way of building and thinking. It proposes an open system based on a customizable set of elements: frames, cartridges, blocks, fixtures, equipment, and furnishings.

Our firm is collaborating with LivingHomes, a Santa Monica—based developer of "housing products."

As a new kind of player operating within the design and construction industry, they are acting neither as developer, designer, nor builder. Developers typically package land, infrastructure, and entitlements; designers transform program into form and provide instructions to contractors; and builders implement the program that has been handed over to them. LivingHomes works between these entities and the site's owners. Their tactic is to direct developers and would-be homeowners to a customized endproduct, which the LivingHomes design team will adapt to given circumstances of climate, place, and budget.

As architects, we share several ideals in common with LivingHomes, including the desire to provide high-quality dwellings that are well designed, environmentally responsible, and affordable. The housing products they offer are fabricated off site and incorporate sustainable design elements to the greatest extent possible. For them, we have developed both single- and multi-family homes from research that originated with Loblolly House. Our multi-family product employs a cartridge system with an integrated structure that eliminates the need for a traditional frame. The cartridges, which are fabricated out of light-gauge steel or wood, are used in a variety of locations, including for the roof, floors, exterior walls, interior partitions, and core service panels. Wall cartridges are two-story, balloon-framed elements with floor cartridges attached at the base. Exterior cladding materials include stucco, cement board, vertical siding, parklex, lap siding, stained wood, metal paneling, and standing seams. Bathrooms, kitchens, and mechanical rooms are formed as blocks: singular units enclosing system-intensive spaces. Our proposal for LivingHomes is an effort to bring mass-customized ecological housing to a demographic that, until now, has been excluded from the market.

At the same time that we were pursuing the implementation of a commercial model based on the ideals articulated in Loblolly House, we were also engaged in research to develop a case study house commissioned by the Museum of Modern Art for its 2008 exhibition, *Home Delivery*. Cellophane House is an 1,800-square-foot aluminum-frame dwelling. On the first level are a car port and mechanical room. The second level accommodates living, dining, and kitchen functions; bedrooms

with baths and closets are located on the third and fourth levels. All of the walls, floors, and even the roof are either transparent or translucent. Cellophane House advances several aspects of the Loblolly House agenda: speed of on-site assembly, design for full disassembly, and a holistic approach to the life cycles of materials (using recycled and recyclable sources), as well as further development of the high-performance building skin first articulated in our SmartWrap Pavillion, commissioned for an exhibition at the Cooper Hewitt National Design Museum in 2004.

Cellophane House takes Loblolly House's "foundation-up" approach to scheduling one step further by collapsing the duration of on-site assembly from six weeks to one. The tactic for accomplishing this duration is increased off-site assembly and integration. Owing to the house's small footprint, there were additional opportunities for developing single-story prefabricated blocks for the front and rear portions. The entire rear of the house forms an eight-foot-wide by twenty-foot-long block containing structural plastic stairs and floor panels, a hallway, and an integrated photovoltaic curtainwall system. The front wall of the house also forms a twenty-foot-wide block with an integrated curtainwall composed of operable panels for managing cross-ventilation. Using these fully assembled front and rear blocks as bookend-like scaffolds, the entire middle section of the house is then installed as a flat-panel system with plastic floors fastened to aluminum beams. Like Loblolly House, the Cellophane House relies on a hybrid system of blocks and panels, but it shifts the ratio to more spatial blocks and fewer panels. Instead of thermal mass, Cellophane House uses a multi-layer skin to produce energy and filter solar gain. Photovoltaic film is integrated into the glazing on the south-facing wall and roof canopy. A layer of photovoltaic film is also encased within inner and outer layers of the sidewall panels made of polyethylene terephthalate (PET) plastic. It is estimated that this building-integrated photovoltaic system can produce enough energy to meet the house's basic electrical needs. Lastly, placed between the sidewall's PET layers is an ultraviolet-filtering film that mitigates unwanted heat gain while the inner cavity functions as a solar chimney, allowing warm air to rise and exit through a vent on the roof (in summer) or, when the vent is closed, for a heat-blanket to form around the building envelope (in winter). Cellophane House seeks to combine fully reclaimable and recyclable materials with enhanced energy performance—achieved through better integration of the building skin—within a customizable lightweight structure.

We want change, not another prototype. The real measure of the success or failure of Loblolly House lies in its process. If the hybrid system of off-site fabrication and on-site assembly that we have developed yields changes in the housing supply-chain—with a new breed of suppliers beginning to provide integrated assemblies for the industry at-large and with builders using the elements to develop affordable, high-quality housing with a reduced environmental footprint—then this little house will have succeeded as an instigator of change.

LivingHomes

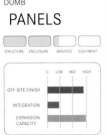

DUMB

PANELS

STRUCTURE ENCLOSURE SERVICES EQUIPMENT

	0	LOW	MID	HIGH
OFF-SITE FINISH				
INTEGRATION				
EXPANSION CAPACITY				

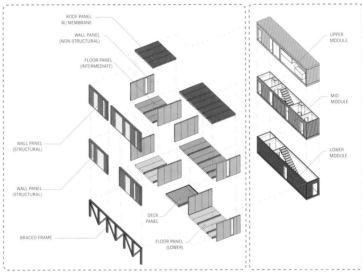

ROOF PANEL
W/MEMBRANE

WALL PANEL
(NON-STRUCTURAL)

FLOOR PANEL
(INTERMEDIATE)

WALL PANEL
(STRUCTURAL)

WALL PANEL
(STRUCTURAL)

BRACED FRAME

DECK
PANEL

FLOOR PANEL
(LOWER)

UPPER
MODULE

MID
MODULE

LOWER
MODULE

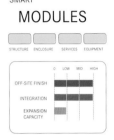

SMART

MODULES

STRUCTURE ENCLOSURE SERVICES EQUIPMENT

	0	LOW	MID	HIGH
OFF-SITE FINISH				
INTEGRATION				
EXPANSION CAPACITY				

8.1

8.1
Deconstructed diagram of KieranTimberlake's
LivingHomes prototype

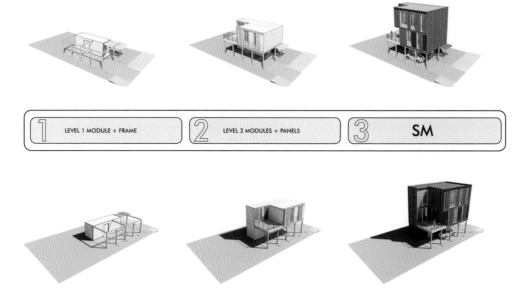

| 1 | LEVEL 1 MODULE + FRAME | 2 | LEVEL 2 MODULES + PANELS | 3 | SM |

8.2

8.2
Size variants and configurations of
LivingHomes prototype

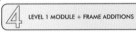

4 LEVEL 1 MODULE + FRAME ADDITIONS

5 MED

6 LG

COR-TEN STEEL PANEL

HORIZONTAL CORRUGATED STEEL
WITH CEMENT BOARD

CORRUGATED ALUMINUM

TRESPA METEON

HORIZONTAL CEDAR SIDING

LAP SIDING

PARKLEX

CORRUGATED POWDER
COATED METAL

TWO-TONE PARKLEX

TWO-TONE TRESPA METEON

VERTICAL WOOD SIDING

CORRUGATED COR-TEN STEEL

8.3

8.3
Cladding and configuration options of
LivingHomes prototype

Cellophane House

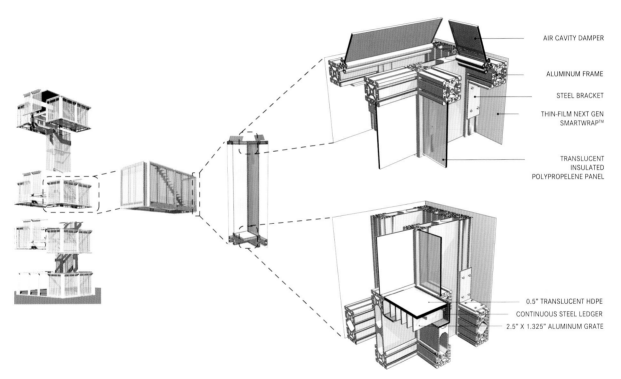

AIR CAVITY DAMPER

ALUMINUM FRAME

STEEL BRACKET

THIN-FILM NEXT GEN SMARTWRAP™

TRANSLUCENT INSULATED POLYPROPELENE PANEL

0.5" TRANSLUCENT HDPE
CONTINUOUS STEEL LEDGER
2.5" X 1.325" ALUMINUM GRATE

9.1

9.1
Deconstructed diagram of Cellophane House,
a concept dwelling commissioned by the
Museum of Modern Art, 2008

COMPONENT	Frame	Skin	Glazing
MATERIAL	Bosch Aluminum Framing / Steel Connectors	PET Film	Aluminum Frame IGU
CODE	AL / STEEL	1 PETE	Glass Recycles
WEIGHT	10,504 LBS aluminum 200 LBS steel	170 LBS	2,033 LBS
RECYCLABLE MASS	26%	0.4%	5%

9.2

9.2
Matrix of off-the-shelf components and their
associated waste and recycling streams

Wall Panels	Window Frames	Floors	Roof	Stairs
8mm Polypropylene Sheet	Aluminum Frame	Aluminum Grate / 0.5" Polyethylene Sheet	Greengrid System / Aluminum Grate / 3.5" (R25) Rigid Polyisocyanate / Adhered EPDM	Aluminum Grate
PP (5)	AL	AL / HDPE (2)	AL	AL
1373 LBS	260 LBS	9797 LBS aluminum / 4587 LBS polyethylene	6900 LBS greengrid / 2898 LBS aluminum / 207 LBS polyisocyanate / 187 LBS epdm	2,040 LBS
3%	0.6%	35%	7%	5%

TOTAL RECYCLABLE MASS = 82%

9.3

9.3
Rendering of a multi-family complex in an urban setting

9.4
Rendering of a single-family home in a rural setting

9.5
Elements of the hybrid housing system

9.4

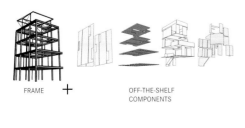

FRAME   **+**   OFF-THE-SHELF
COMPONENTS

$$$

$

CUSTOMIZABLE
OPTIONS:
SHELL
INTERIORS
SERVICES
EQUIPMENT

9.5

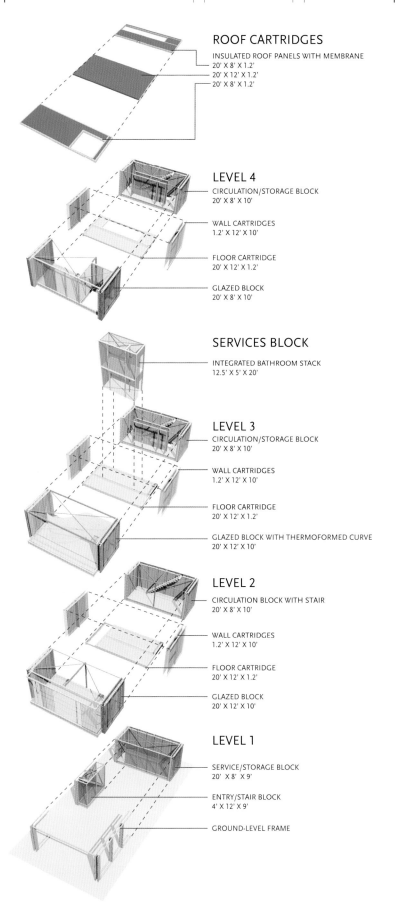

ROOF CARTRIDGES

INSULATED ROOF PANELS WITH MEMBRANE
20' X 8' X 1.2'
20' X 12' X 1.2'
20' X 8' X 1.2'

LEVEL 4

CIRCULATION/STORAGE BLOCK
20' X 8' X 10'

WALL CARTRIDGES
1.2' X 12' X 10'

FLOOR CARTRIDGE
20' X 12' X 1.2'

GLAZED BLOCK
20' X 8' X 10'

SERVICES BLOCK

INTEGRATED BATHROOM STACK
12.5' X 5' X 20'

LEVEL 3

CIRCULATION/STORAGE BLOCK
20' X 8' X 10'

WALL CARTRIDGES
1.2' X 12' X 10'

FLOOR CARTRIDGE
20' X 12' X 1.2'

GLAZED BLOCK WITH THERMOFORMED CURVE
20' X 12' X 10'

LEVEL 2

CIRCULATION BLOCK WITH STAIR
20' X 8' X 10'

WALL CARTRIDGES
1.2' X 12' X 10'

FLOOR CARTRIDGE
20' X 12' X 1.2'

GLAZED BLOCK
20' X 12' X 10'

LEVEL 1

SERVICE/STORAGE BLOCK
20' X 8' X 9'

ENTRY/STAIR BLOCK
4' X 12' X 9'

GROUND-LEVEL FRAME

9.6
On-site assembly diagram

9.7
Evening rendering

Afterword

James Timberlake

Piles: the kind used in foundations. How we chose to use them. How they came to be deployed. And the process of installing them. Do we grid them? Attempt to drive them at an angle, or have them all line up? Do we finish them or let them be expressed for what they truly are? Formally, what is the best solution? Can we experiment? With our apologies to Louis Kahn, what does a pile *want* to be?

Elevating Loblolly House was a necessity to protect it from the flooding tides that occasionally disfigure the site's graceful shoreline along the Chesapeake Bay. Lifting it up reaped immediate benefits. More importantly, though, as in all of our work, the decision to deploy piles required that we meet more than one criterion. We always strive for four or five criteria to be solved in every decision. First, the piles offered protection from the tides. Second, the overhang provided a sheltered space for a car, a necessary amenity when arriving and departing from this remote site. Third, the height of the house allowed us to capture the site's prevailing water-to-land breezes and made for more pleasant living. Fourth, the

living space was immediately enhanced by the spectacular views of the bay and surrounding landscape. Lastly, in an homage to Le Corbusier and Richard Neutra, placing the house on lowbrow *piloti*—highbrow would have been concrete, not wood—ensured a connection to the modernist legacy. The piles represented our passport beyond the mundane.

Fast forward to months and months later when the pile driver and crew were on site. Having attempted to drive several piles askew to the grid and a few degrees off from perpendicular, our lowbrow *piloti* were in splinters. Sitting with the frustrated pile driver, we were asking ourselves, where do we go from here? Formally, the piles *wanted* to be straight. After all, trees grow straight, not skewed, and generally not in a strict grid formation, except perhaps loblolly pines. These, however, were already spread throughout the site. A pile didn't want to be just a decapitated loblolly. The house was to be an extension of the forest, but clearly we were not in grid territory and certainly not in straight up-and-down turf. After many weeks and some amount of expended capital—both the money and the goodwill kinds—the pile driver and semifulfilled operator were leaving the site, with most of the piles having been driven at normative angles to the earth and just a few offset and angled. The foreman was muttering to himself about architects, plans, BIMs, and, most dreadful of all, collaboration. The pile driver and operator knew of only one way, straight up and down, and please do not ask to do it any other way. The architects and owner wanted a certain, other way. Yet again, we were asking ourselves, *where do we go from here*?

That statement—the title of several talks that Steve and I recently gave regarding our research and work—aptly applies to our efforts upon the completion of Loblolly House. Back in 2005, when Steve first suggested that he and Barbara wanted to build a retreat on a recently acquired parcel of property near the Chesapeake, the challenge of *where do we go* was clear. This was an opportunity to build, literally and figuratively—to test the concepts we had advocated in *Refabricating Architecture*—and to see our ideas realized in a project controlled, directed, designed, enabled, and integrated by us. Our research, our search, was not just to find answers to the questions of what things wanted to be, but to find solutions to the processes of how things came to be. Perfection was our ideal, in less time, with more collaboration, and with fewer mistakes.

By 2007, our ideas and ideals had mostly come true, as chronicled within the pages in this book. A beautiful retreat exists. The messy vitality of on-site construction, which would have made a wreck of the site, gave way to off-site fabrication. Our vision of reorganizing the construction paradigm was mostly achieved, if only for the split second it took to build this house. Our goals for quality were met, possibly even exceeded in some instances, if only for a singular house customized to the owners' needs. But questions lingered. What had we learned from the piles and what lies above them?

As a profession and an industry we must learn to embrace change or accept the consequences of declining productivity, decreasing affordability, and increasing irrelevance to a majority of those who want to construct shelter. Irrelevance is worse than extinction. One toils for what purpose? Extinction, at least, holds historical significance. Change is inevitable, and we see the harbingers of it all around us. Our clients demand it. Our consultants desire it. Accepting change moves us from the heaps of wreckage and uncertainty of piles to producing architecture for the world above, that of cartridges, grand blocks, and integrated component assemblies. Precise, clean, and orderly, but not without internal complexities, Loblolly House offers a way forward. It represents change.

As with the rest of our work, the process that led to Loblolly House was one that rejected the notion of a conventional language of modern design. Rather than begin from the premise of a certain look being the principal driver of composition, we subscribe to an open, holistic process of need and solution. We reject what many architects constitute as an important result. We do not adhere to a formal language, requiring that construction support appearance, inside or out. Rather, the appearance is the result of carefully constructed decisions, interwoven in search of solutions and guided by the ultimate objective of placing substance over surface. We believe that beauty is inherent in all things and that it resides in whatever composition has been carefully constructed of informed

solutions. Are the piles ugly or beautiful? We think of them as beautiful, but in different circumstances they may have been ugly. As Michael Stacey suggests in the introduction to this book, architects need to uninvent the process that has led to the current state of design. A new ecology of architecture must emerge, with sustainable solutions driven by performance, not appearance. A new order of beauty, derived from purposeful deployment, will become the new language, the *new polemic*.

Loblolly House was a private effort to address a very public issue: that the way architects design and contractors build is hopelessly broken. It was an attempt to find hope in the future and in the changes that will soon overwhelm us all. To those afraid of a future unlike that we were trained for, consider Franklin Delano Roosevelt's advice at the advent of World War II: "The only thing we have to fear is fear itself." Further construction doom notwithstanding, these fears—of BIM, of collaboration, of losing control, of abdicating our roles as architects to those who wield hammers and saws—were unfounded. Instead, we encountered allies in all aspects of design and construction, from engineers to contractors, suppliers to

assemblers, and architecture interns to apprentice crafts-
men. Even in our hapless pile-driving foreman, we found
an ally. We decided to make our private effort, our experiment, public in order to address those fears and dispel
the critics who said it could not be done.

That we could not improve design and construction.
That we could not improve the supply chain.
That we could not do better.

Nonsense.

Appendix
3-D Fly-through

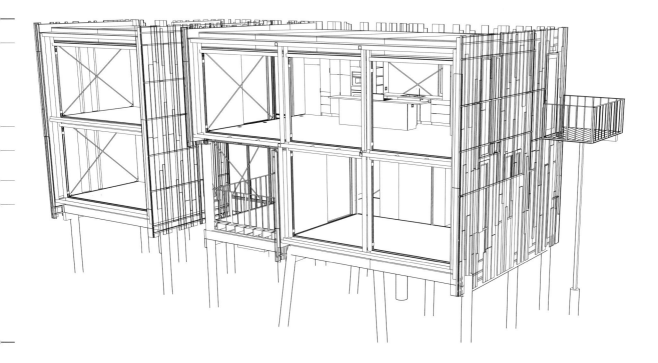

10.1
View from southwest, with adjustable facade
doors removed

10.2
View of exterior staircase, from northeast

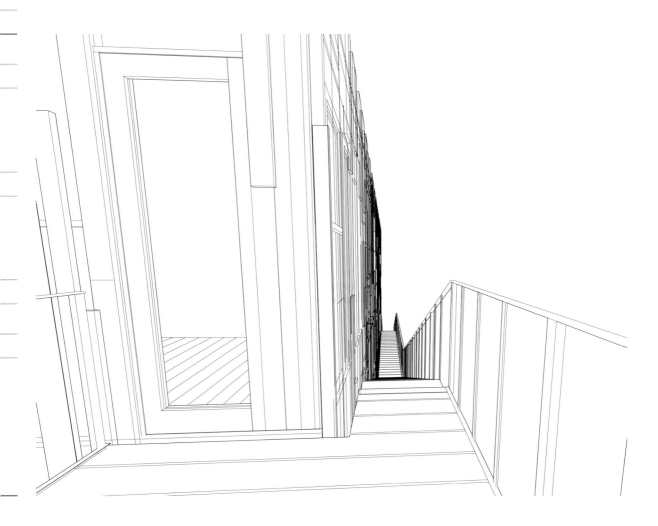

10.3
View of main entrance on second level

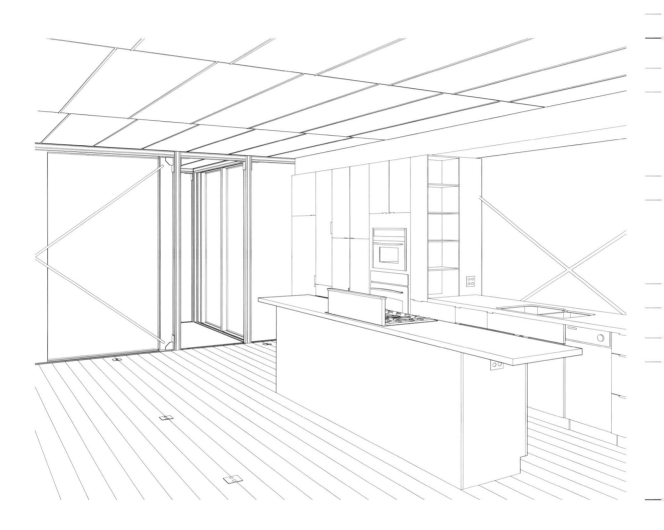

10.4
Interior view from kitchen to glass footbridge,
second level

10.5
View of footbridge from second-level guest wing

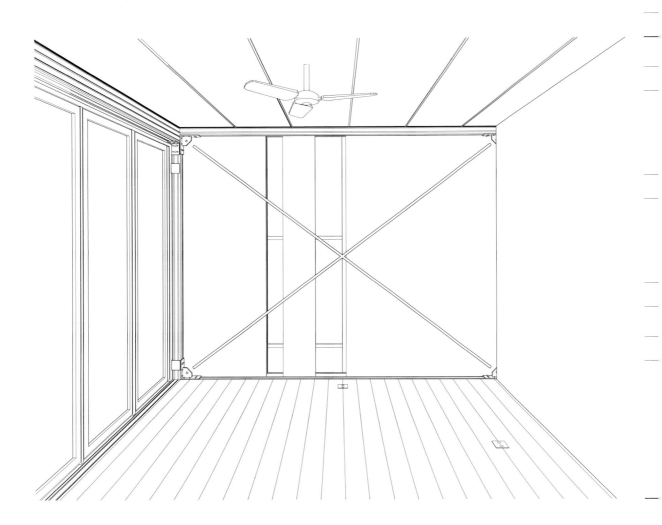

10.6
Guest room, second level

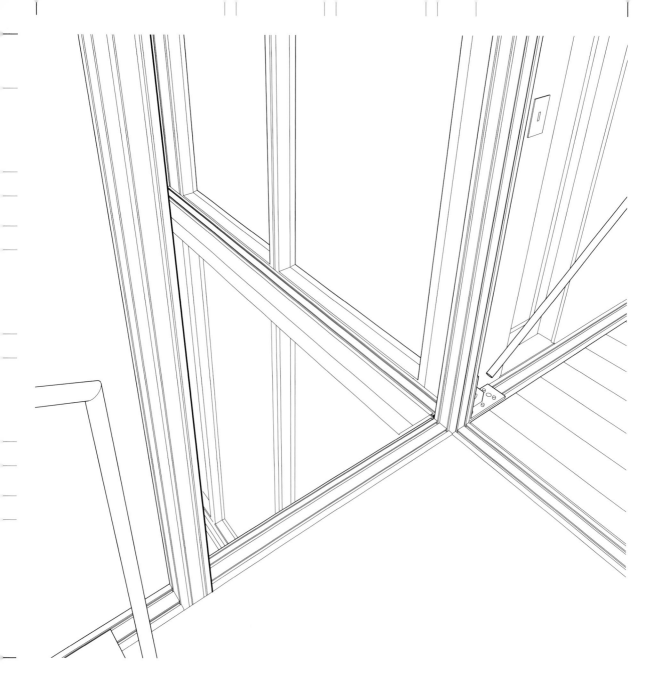

10.7
Detail of scaffold at upper landing of interior
spiral staircase, second level

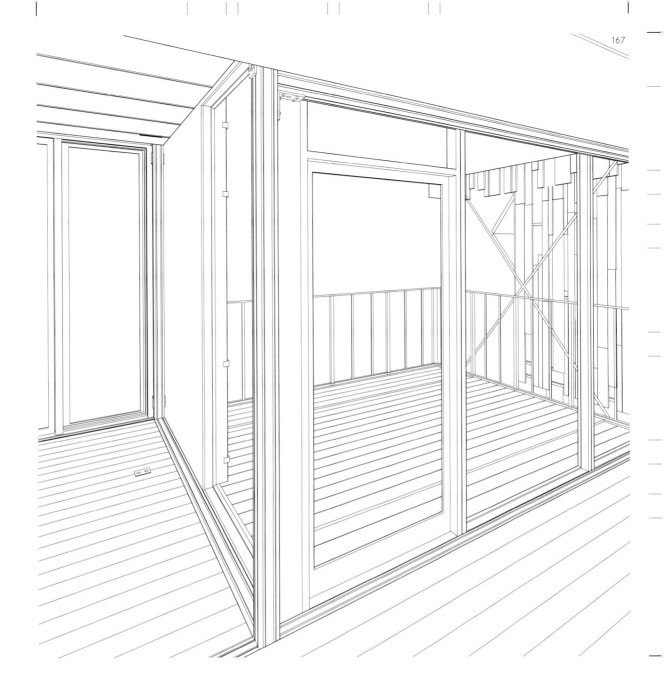

10.8
Covered porch viewed from hallway, first level

10.9
View to covered porch from inside the master
bedroom, first level

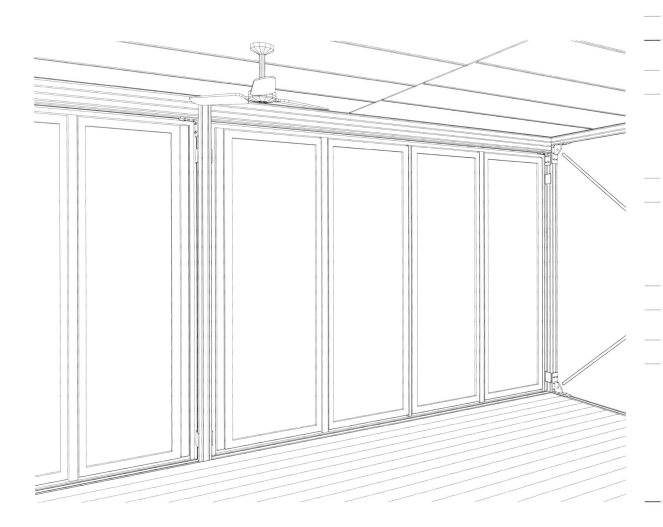

10.10
Interior view of bifolding glass doors, first level

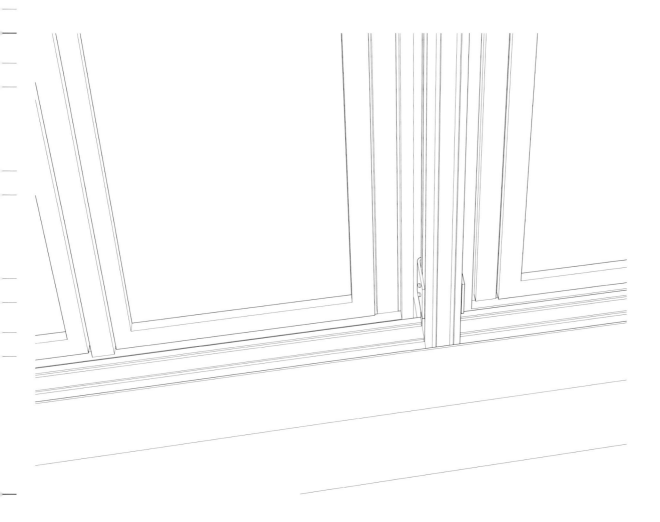

10.11
Detail of aluminum frame and bifolding doors

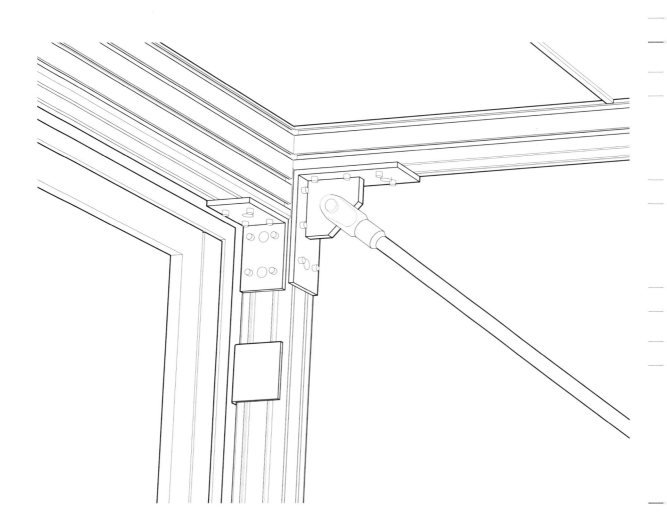

10.12
Detail of diagonal bracing connector

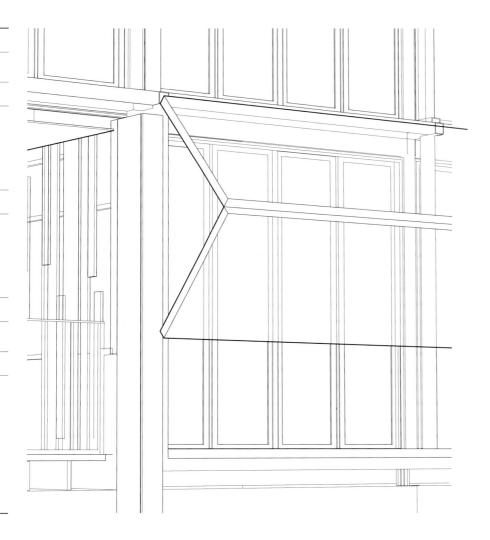

10.13
Exterior detail of bifolding facade

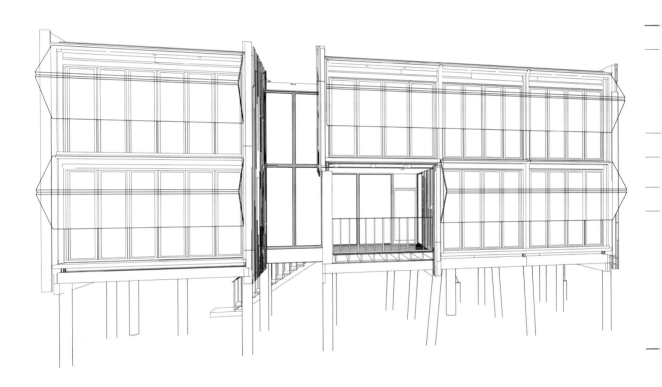

10.14
View from west

Acknowledgments

While it all began with a desire for a summerhome, our original impulse for building Loblolly House—beyond the uncommonly special site—was our previous book, *Refabricating Architecture,* published in 2003. Though Loblolly House is foremost a home, it is also an experiment. It is the literal construction of a theory, a test of an ideal. First, my wife Barbara Degrange Kieran embraced this process. For this act of faith, no thanks can suffice. We owe thanks to the AIA College of Fellows, who awarded us their first Latrobe Prize, without which the research that led to the publication of our previous book may not have begun. Since there would be no *Loblolly House: Elements of a New Architecture* without there first being a house, we owe special thanks to all of the people who engaged in the process of its design, fabrication, and assembly. In our office, David Riz directed the project from start to finish; Mark Rhodes, Jeff Goldstein, and George Ristow initiated the work. Marilia Rodrigues, having inherited the project from them, compelled us all—owner, suppliers, off-site fabricators, and on-site assemblers—to move forward in ways none could have imagined at the outset. Without her talent, skill, unwavering confidence, and good humor, the experiment that is Loblolly House would not have come to pass. Shawn Protz and Alexandra Gauzza assisted Marilia along the way. Tedd Benson of Bensonwood Homes agreed to do what no other fabricator would consider: craft and erect a house consisting almost entirely of integrated component assemblies. Paul Boa, Hans Porschitz, and Anthony Poanessa, also of Bensonwood Homes, transformed our intentions into a comprehensive model, building the house virtually and giving us the confidence to fabricate its elements in advance of assembly. Chip Arena, of Arena Program Management, and his project manager Mark Anthony willingly tread the murky waters of this new process, performing all site-based construction and installation. Within our office, Carin Whitney directed the assembly of text and illustrations for this book. Shawn Protz, Jeff Cumpson, and Casey Boss assisted her along the way, preparing the graphics. At Princeton Architectural Press, our editor Laurie Manfra transformed a manuscript generated in the seams of life, on trains and in planes, into a cohesive synthesis of theory and practice.